LAKE DISTRICT ICONS

PEOPLE, PLACES AND THINGS THAT MAKE CUMBRIA GREAT

MICHAELA ROBINSON-TATE & PHIL RIGBY

For
Jack and Leo
Kezia and Leo
Lucie and Rosie

All photographs taken by Phil Rigby

First published 2014

The History Press
The Mill, Brimscombe Port
Stroud, Gloucestershire, GL5 2QG
www.thehistorypress.co.uk

© Michaela Robinson-Tate and Phil Rigby, 2014

The right of Michaela Robinson-Tate and Phil Rigby to be identified
as the Authors of this work has been asserted in accordance with the
Copyright, Designs and Patents Act 1988.

British Library Cataloguing in Publication Data.
A catalogue record for this book is available from the British Library.

ISBN 978 0 7509 5910 0

Typesetting and origination by The History Press and Printed in Malta by Melita Press
Production managed by Jellyfish

CONTENTS

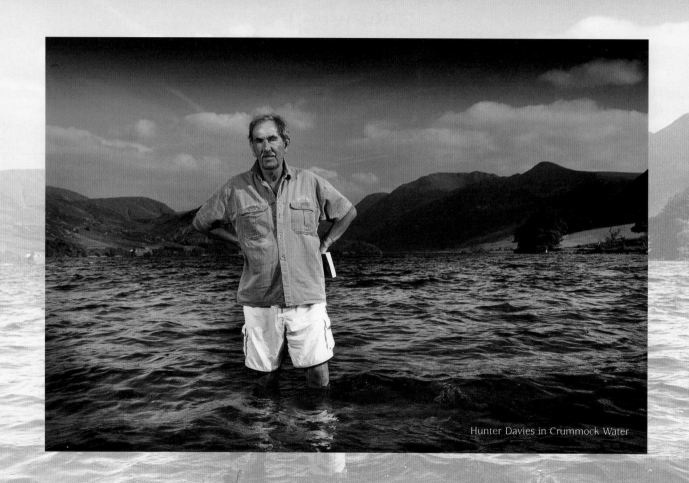

Hunter Davies in Crummock Water

FOREWORD

IT'S A PRETTY MEANINGLESS, devalued, rubbish accolade these days to describe anyone as an icon. Every TV weather forecaster, lumpen Premiership player, lingerie model and soap actress gets referred to at some time as an icon, even if it's just in their own publicity handouts.

Originally it had a religious connotation – from the Greek, meaning image – and referred to a small image, usually a painting on wood, of a religious subject. Today it means the image of anyone really, anyone whom some of us can vaguely recognise or even vaguely worship; for we live in an age when being any sort of celebrity appears to be a cause for admiration.

So well done to Michaela and Phil for attempting to resurrect the word and the concept of an icon as an object which is truly worth worshipping. Not necessarily down-on-the-knees worshipping, though personally I would always take my cap off, if I wore one, to the blessed Wainwright. But a nod of the head and a murmur of the lips sort of homage is surely permissible for those whom they have decided in their wisdom and knowledge are Lake District icons.

And what a rich field they have to choose from. For we are indeed blessed in Cumbria that in such a small geographical space we have so much. Wordsworth was one of the first to spot this, as he wrote in his *Guide to the Lakes* which dates back to 1810: 'I do not know any tract of country in which, in so narrow a compass may be found an equal variety in the influence of light and shade upon the sublime and beautiful features.'

He was writing about nature, thinking about the landscape, but it also applies to people and things. One of the interesting aspects of our landscape is that it has attracted so many famous people, natives and others, who have wanted to live here, do things here, create things here. I can't think of another small patch of the globe which has inspired so many people and produced such a variety of ideas and creations over such a long period.

Wordsworth was a real native, but neither Wainwright nor Beatrix Potter was born here. They just wanted to be here, breathe in here, pass on what had inspired them to millions of others around the world.

I like the fact that Michaela and Phil have chosen just as many things and places amongst their icons as people. We can look up to lakes and sheep just as much as to certain folks. And of course I love Phil's wonderful photographs, icons in themselves, which make you pause and wonder.

You will probably disagree with some of the choices. (I for one can't believe that for one second they or anyone can possibly imagine that the person in Chapter 4 is an icon, issa joke, shurely.) Or more likely, you will think of loads of other people and things equally deserving who should have been included here. Ah well, that could give them another book, when this sells out …

Hunter Davies, 2014

INTRODUCTION AND ACKNOWLEDGEMENTS

L AKE DISTRICT ICONS is our fan letter to the place where we're privileged to work. During 2012 and its washout summer and 2013, when the sun shone more than it didn't, we travelled around Cumbria to meet experts on subjects as diverse as Kendal Mint Cake, John Ruskin and the Lake District's most challenging high mountain passes. This book, which features more than eighty previously unpublished photographs and original research, is the result.

Icons is an overused word but we believe it encapsulates the qualities of our chosen subjects. All of them are, in some way, symbols of the Lake District and are known and admired nationally and even across the world. We wanted to take a fresh look at these figures and the places and things that make Cumbria such a fascinating place. We didn't set out to provide a definitive account of our icons but rather to offer a sideways and hopefully entertaining take on Cumbria's culture.

We met living icons, such as the climbers Chris Bonington, Dave Birkett and Leo Houlding and the writers and commentators Hunter Davies and Melvyn Bragg. Judith Notley spent a day helping us to bring Beatrix Potter to life, as you can see in Chapter 8. We travelled to her home near Leeds to visit Gina Campbell, forever linked with the Lake District after the death of her father, Donald Campbell, when his Bluebird boat crashed on Coniston Water. We spoke to the Beatrix Potter biographer Linda Lear at her home in the USA. No one we approached for help turned us down and we're grateful to them all.

We couldn't have written *Lake District Icons* without Judy Rigby and Andy Tate, who we thank for their unstinting support and their patience. We are grateful to Richard Eccles, publishing director/editor of *Cumbria Life* and CN Magazines, where we work, for his help and enthusiasm from the beginning. Thank you to Matilda Richards and The History Press, for seeing the worth of *Lake District Icons* and to our editor, Ruth Boyes, for her care and attention to detail. Hunter Davies was kind enough not only to submit to an interview and photographs but also to provide a foreword, for which we are very grateful. John Williams put himself out to help with the Scafells chapter. Michaela would like to thank her parents, Peter and Marie Robinson, for their encouragement. Thank you to Dr Michael Greaney and Dr Andrew Tate for proofreading; any mistakes are our own. For interviews and photographs we are indebted to: Professor Simon Bainbridge; Will and Sam Rawling; Bill Birkett; Lord (Melvyn) Bragg; Hunter Davies; Eric Robson; Kendal Museum and the Wainwright Estate; Jane King; Shane and John Barron; Museum of Lakeland Life and Industry in Kendal and Lakeland Arts Trust; Nick Thorne; Dr Linda Lear; Willow Taylor; Judith Notley (www.thebeatrixpottershow.co.uk); Sir Chris Bonington; Dave Birkett; Leo Houlding; Professor Stephen Wildman; Howard Hull; Harry Berger and family; Kevin Wrathall and family; Gina Campbell QSO and Vicky Slowe.

Note: before we receive any angry letters, we should add that we realise not all of the county of Cumbria is within the national park. We use the names Lake District and Cumbria interchangeably for the sake of simplicity.

Michaela Robinson-Tate and Phil Rigby, 2014

CHAPTER 1

WILLIAM WORDSWORTH

WILLIAM WORDSWORTH was an adolescent graffiti artist. He was still a pupil at Hawkshead Grammar School when he developed a taste for gouging his initials into significant objects around him. The schoolboy William took a knife – probably the one used to sharpen his quill pen – to his oak desk and hacked in the legend 'W Wordsworth'. The autograph has become such a focal point for the thousands of visitors to the building each year that it has been fitted with a transparent cover to prevent the letters from being rubbed away.

Years later and William the graffitist was still at it but by this time he'd moved on to the great outdoors. A slab of stone on the road alongside Thirlmere, now known as the Rock of Names, was defaced with the letters WW as well as the initials of the poet's sister Dorothy and brother John, his wife Mary Hutchinson, Mary's sister Sara and Wordsworth's fellow poet and friend Samuel Taylor Coleridge. Today the rock, with the initials still clearly visible, can be found in the garden of Dove Cottage, Wordsworth's former home at Grasmere.

That sense of the poet wanting to own the landscape around him extended beyond graffiti. Wordsworth wrote a series of verses – *Poems on the Naming of Places* – in which the names of members of his circle were given to landscape features, either because they were associated or shared characteristics with the spot. In one of these we learn that his sister, Dorothy, named a 'lonely summit' above Grasmere after William. The rocky outcrop in question, Stone Arthur, is said in the poem to often send its 'own deep quiet to restore our hearts', giving an indication of Dorothy's strong admiration for her brother. Apart from marking out

Wordsworth as a bit of a delinquent, these acts of vandalism and later the *Naming of Places* series, show the poet wanting to make his mark – literally as well as in a literary way – on the Lake District. He was so successful in doing so that today, 160 years after his death, the name Wordsworth is synonymous with the Lake District. As Melvyn Bragg puts it: 'If any place in England is the literary property of one man, then that property is Cumbria and that man is William Wordsworth.' Dickens' London, Jane Austen's Bath and even Shakespeare's Stratford can't compete with the affinity that the poet has with the Lake District. Simon Bainbridge, Professor of Romantic Studies at Lancaster University, says: 'There's no other writer who's quite as associated with a single place as Wordsworth is and I think that's partly because his own writing seeks to make the place his own and he seeks to understand himself as a writer through locating himself in a specific place.'

Wordsworth's Cumbrian credentials have never been in doubt. Unlike two other Lake District literary figures, John Ruskin and Beatrix Potter, Wordsworth was no offcomer. He was born and brought up in Cockermouth, educated at Hawkshead and spent much of his adult life in Grasmere and Rydal. But his life didn't run as smoothly as this history implies. The deaths of his parents meant there was disruption for the family and an enforced separation between Wordsworth and his only sister, Dorothy. In his 20s, he lived a nomadic life in Cambridge, London, Somerset and France. He was about to turn 30 in late 1799 when he and Dorothy were able to set up house together in Grasmere and it was an important homecoming for the poet. He wrote about it in 'Home at Grasmere',

In Wordsworth's Poems on the Naming of Places, *we learn that Dorothy Wordsworth chose Stone Arthur, overlooking Grasmere village, to represent her brother*

a poem in which he remembers how, as a boy, he was roaming the Lake District hills and found himself on Loughrigg Terrace. Looking down on Grasmere, he had a vision that showed him it was where he wanted to be. Twenty years later, when he and Dorothy moved to Grasmere together, it fulfilled that vision and helped to give him his sense of poetic vocation. The way in which Wordsworth, Dorothy and Coleridge worked as a team, writing together, reading and discussing their poetry, also gave him a sense of stability he hadn't had before.

He felt protected by the landscape around him. In his great autobiographical poem *The Prelude* he wrote about how nature had taken on a parental role and fostered him: 'Fair seed-time had my soul, and I grew up / Fostered alike by beauty and by fear.' Although Wordsworth would have written poetry wherever he settled, Simon Bainbridge believes there was something about the mountainous landscape of the Lake District which became important in his writing. He says: 'I think it's hard to imagine him writing the work that he goes on to write had he not been back in the specific location of the Lakes.'

By the time the Wordsworths moved to their final home, Rydal Mount, in 1812, the poet had become a tourist attraction in his own right. People began to call on him at the house and he was – understandably – annoyed when visitors took things from the garden as souvenirs. In his book *Wordsworth and the Lake District*, David McCracken says that by the early nineteenth century, the Lake District had become a popular destination but visitors came to see the poet as well as the country he wrote about. In fact, hundreds of strangers arrived each summer on what the essayist Charles Lamb called gaping missions.

Ask someone today what they most associate with Wordsworth and chances are they'll say 'Daffodils', the popular name for his poem 'I Wandered Lonely as a Cloud'. 'Daffodils' has only become what is possibly Wordsworth's defining work since his death and a nice irony is that he wrote three poems about the common pilewort or celandine. Perhaps unsurprisingly, the tourist industry in Cumbria hasn't latched on to spring sightings of the humble 'Wordsworth's common pilewort' as a potential magnet for visitors.

Wordsworth, his sister Dorothy and their circle, carved their initials into a stone slab, now known as the Rock of Names

In 'Home at Grasmere', Wordsworth wrote about this view from Loughrigg Terrace and how he'd had a vision that this was where he wanted to be

However, during his lifetime, Wordsworth's fame was partly based on a book that had nothing to do with his poetry. Wordsworth's *A Guide through the District of the Lakes*, as it was eventually called, or just *Guide to the Lakes* was – as the title suggests – essentially a guidebook. It first appeared in print in 1810 and was republished in a number of editions, becoming very successful. In fact, the man who was to become Poet Laureate was so well known for the *Guide* that he was once famously asked by a clergyman if he'd written anything else. As well as offering travel advice in the *Guide*, Wordsworth took the opportunity to rail against the planting of non-native trees, obtrusive new homes and the whitewashing of cottages and wrote: 'The author has been induced to speak thus at length, by a wish to preserve the native beauty of this delightful district, because still further changes in its appearance must inevitably follow, from the change of inhabitants and owners which is rapidly taking place.' Anticipating the formation of the national park by about 140 years, he also wrote about the Lake District as 'a sort of national property'. However, he must have been aware of the irony that the popularity of the Lakes as a holiday destination and as a place to aspire to move to, had in part been fed by his own fame and the focus on the Lakes in both his poems and his *Guide*. Simon Bainbridge believes that he would have been aware that he had played a 'significant role in the popularisation of the Lake District'.

Despite his view of it as 'national property', Wordsworth didn't appear to believe that the Lake District should be open to everyone. At the start of the *Guide* he says that he has written it as a companion for the 'minds of persons of taste, and feeling for Landscape'.

By 1844, his views appear to have become quite severe. In a letter to *The Morning Post* objecting to the proposed Kendal and Windermere Railway, he said that the Lake District could only be properly enjoyed by a mind 'disposed to peace'. The letter recommended that anyone who wanted noisy pleasure should go to a pantomime, a farce or a puppet-show. He went on: 'But may those who have given proof that they prefer other gratifications continue to be safe from the molestation of cheap trains pouring out their hundreds at a time along the margin of Windermere.' Wordsworth thought the railway would be disastrous for the landscape that he loved. In a separate letter to the newspaper he wrote: 'Consider also the state of the Lake district; and look, in the first place, at the little town of Bowness, in the event of such railway inundations. What would become of it in this, not the Retreat, but the Advance, of the Ten Thousand? […] Alas, alas, if the lakes are to pay this penalty for their own attractions!'

Wordsworth sounds like a man who wanted to keep the Lake District for himself and his friends and who didn't believe that other people would be able to appreciate it properly. However, Simon Bainbridge says there are more sympathetic ways of reading Wordsworth's objections than merely to regard him as a snob who doesn't want the growing lower middle classes to experience the Lake District. 'He's genuinely interested

Wild daffodils in Dora's Field at Rydal – Wordsworth wrote about the flower in his best-known poem, 'I Wandered Lonely as a Cloud'

in preserving the physical environment; that's something you can see through the *Guide*,' he says. 'I suppose for him the coming of the railways represented a quickening of the pace of life which he finds difficult to reconcile with a more steady relationship with the natural world.'

Simon also says that between the first edition of the *Guide* in 1810, and Wordsworth's letters objecting to the railways in 1843, there had been a great deal of change, with more and more people coming to the Lakes. Although when Wordsworth began his *Guide* the Lakes had been a fashionable destination for tours for some time, it wasn't until near the end of his life that the age of mass tourism really arrived. Thomas Cook started his travel company in 1841 – just three years before Wordsworth's anti-railway rants. It would appear that Wordsworth had become a grumpy old man.

Despite Wordsworth's best efforts, the Windermere Railway was opened in 1847. His views about the railway give rise to another irony, because in the Lake District today, many people would be delighted if the line was extended beyond Windermere town to the lake at Bowness-on-Windermere, where it could likely solve many environmental and traffic problems. In fact today, the conservationists who have taken Wordsworth's baton in seeking to protect the landscape would fight to keep a railway in the area, not to prevent one. Despite his concerns about the impact of visitors on the Lakes, Wordsworth's legacy can be seen throughout Cumbria's tourist industry. David McCracken writes: 'Today the Lake District is still, perhaps more strongly than ever, steeped in Wordsworth's presence. His childhood, schoolboy and adult homes are preserved, three of them open to the public and seen by thousands each year instead of by hundreds, as in his day.'

His childhood home in Cockermouth – now called Wordsworth House – Hawkshead Grammar School, Dove Cottage and Rydal Mount can all be visited by the public.

In 2012, the National Trust opened another Wordsworth home, Allan Bank, to paying visitors. Watching it being built, Wordsworth had referred to it as a 'temple of abomination' but he must have managed to overcome his objections for the three years that the family lived there. The addition

Grasmere is a place of pilgrimage for students and lovers of Wordsworth's poems

of Allan Bank means that no fewer than four former homes of one poet, all in one county, are available to the curious tourist.

It's not only Wordsworth's former homes which attract visitors. Cumbria's main tourism organisation has made great play of encouraging holidaymakers to the Lake District in the spring, when they can make the most of 'Wordsworth's daffodils'. It's impossible now to know whether Wordsworth had any idea of the longevity his work and name would achieve, although Simon Bainbridge says he was conscious of his potential literary legacy and the way in which his poems might live on, particularly through other writers. David McCracken believes that Wordsworth was the first writer to take a 'long-range view of the beauty of the Lakes' but we'll also never know if the poet was aware of what a huge role he would play in that long-range view.

What Wordsworth did know was that the Lake District was changing and that he had played a part – for good and ill – in bringing about those changes. He ended his *Guide* by wishing that new homeowners in the Lake District would stick to the 'simplicity and beauty' of the area's existing houses. He also appeared to say that anyone is entitled to enjoy the Lake District, provided they realise what a treasure they have – and presumably take care of it accordingly. In that view, Wordsworth was saying exactly what conservationists are still saying today. As the poet put it:

> In this wish the author will be joined by persons of pure taste throughout the whole island, who, by their visits (often repeated) to the Lakes in the North of England, testify that they deem the district a sort of national property, in which every man has a right and interest who has an eye to perceive and a heart to enjoy.

Grasmere became Wordsworth's home and final resting place

CHAPTER 2

HERDWICKS

IMAGINE THE LAKE DISTRICT fells covered with housing estates. It's a startling image but it's not some dystopian vision of the future dreamed up by government advisers; rather it's a way of describing how Cumbria's native sheep, the Herdwicks, make their home on the high fells.

'It's a bit like a housing estate, with a big area or overall heft and then each family group will have little territories within that heft,' says Herdwick sheep farmer Will Rawling. 'The housing estate is a very good analogy; every family has their own little bit.' Hefting is the name given to the Herdwicks' ability to know where they belong and to return to that place. 'That's a maternal instinct that's passed from mother to daughter and from mother to son,' says Will. 'We can usually find them within about 500 metres of where we would expect to. This is entirely to do with hefting. They're very, very territorial and they all have their little territory within the bigger territory.'

Will has had plenty of opportunity to get to know the behaviour of the hardy Herdwicks. He is chairman of the Herdwick Sheep Breeders' Association – the organisation charged with promoting the breed – and he and his wife, Louise and their son, Sam, farm about 1,200 pure-bred Herdwicks in the Ennerdale Valley in the north-west Lake District. Will's ancestors began breeding Herdwicks in the same location in 1524, making the Rawlings one of the longest-established Herdwick farming families in the Lake District. The Herdwicks themselves have a lengthy history in Cumbria and there is some suggestion that they arrived in the area with Viking invaders. Certainly there is recorded use of the word Herdwyck, meaning sheep pasture, from the twelfth century. They're regarded as the

hardiest of all Britain's hill sheep breeds and can graze on fells of more than 900m or 3,000ft. They are found almost exclusively on 260 farms in Cumbria and the county has 50,000 mature breeding sheep. They've also become something of an unofficial mascot for the Lake District and their image is used on gifts and souvenirs bought by locals and visitors. The shape of their mouths gives them a happy expression. In fact, I've always thought they look as if they're smiling and when I tell Will my theory, he smiles himself: 'They probably are.'

Herdwicks are perfectly suited to life on the fells, having evolved to make the most of the sparse, coarse, high-fibre vegetation that they graze thanks to digestive systems which have been adapted for the task. 'They're very capable of converting vegetation with poor nutritional value into usable proteins and energy,' says Will. The sheep are also able to make the most of more favourable summer conditions, storing up energy for the lean times ahead in brown back fat. Will explains: 'An upland sheep stores energy in its back fat. They use those energy reserves to supplement any nutrition they get from grazing during the winter, to sustain them during that period.' The strong, muscular animals are also very good at foraging and ranging about for their food, which is particularly valuable as they need to eat a lot of the nutritionally poor grass. Not only do their digestive systems work superbly for the conditions but the Herdwicks also benefit from their warm and hard-wearing fleeces, which give them a certain amount of waterproofing – important in an area with high rainfall. 'They can stand anything that the climate can throw at them, other than being buried in the snow,' says Will. Clever sheep, the Herdwicks.

Herdwicks, the Lake District's native sheep breed, are credited with helping to shape the landscape which draws visitors

Herdwicks are not only a familiar sight on the Lake District fells but also integral to how the fells themselves look. Having the hardy sheep grazing in Cumbria's high places prevents the fells from being overtaken by vegetation. Meanwhile, Herdwicks make it possible for farmers to make a living in a place where other types of farming would be impossible, so helping to keep communities alive. However, hill farming has become increasingly challenging over recent years, with farmers struggling to eke out enough profit from their businesses to keep their families. As a consequence, fewer young people want to come into the industry. Against that background, efforts are being made to improve the Herdwick breed's commercial viability. These have included the award of European PDO or Protected Designation of Origin status for Lakeland Herdwick. It means that any meat marketed as such must come from pure-bred sheep which have been born, raised and slaughtered in Lakeland. It's hoped that having the PDO status will help farmers to approach new retailers and restaurants and will add value to the meat. Prince Charles has thrown his weight behind the plans, providing money through his Countryside Fund to help farmers capitalise on the PDO status and find more profitable markets for meat marketed as Herdwick, rather than generic lamb. Herdwick hogget – which is a slightly older lamb – and mutton are also products with good sales potential. Will points out that Herdwick meat is about as extensively reared as it's possible to get, with minimal interference from the farmer. It also has a distinctive taste, thanks to the months that the lambs spend on the fells, maturing slowly and eating the Lake District grass. The tender and gamey meat has also been assessed as containing healthy CLA fats and omega-3 fatty acids and although it's sold at a premium, there's little waste from the carcass. Will says there is a lot that the consumer can learn about the meat: 'It's got a really good story to tell.' The Herdwicks are also important because they give hill farmers the opportunity to produce cross-bred, more productive and commercially viable sheep which they can then sell on, helping to sustain their farms. Although today they're farmed for their meat, at one time the fleece was the most valuable Herdwick product, with the meat eaten as a by-product. The fleeces were so important, in fact, that the proceeds from

▲ *Herdwicks spend most of the year on the high fells, able to fend for themselves through the Lake District winter*

▼ *Tups – the Cumbrian word for rams – being judged at Wasdale*

Herdwick fleeces were once a valuable commodity but today the sheep are farmed principally for their meat

their sale would often pay the farm rent bill. Man-made fibres put an end to that and although Herdwick wool is ideal for carpets and hard-wearing tweed, today the fleeces still command low prices. It often costs a farmer more to shear a sheep than the fleece is worth.

The Herdwick breeding year begins in the middle of November when the ewes are brought down from the fells and sorted into groups with similar-looking types of sheep: for example, darker ewes with others of that colouring and lighter-coloured sheep together. The farmer will match each group with a suitable male sheep or tup, after calculating that their combination of genes will produce the ideal Herdwick with its sought-after slatey-blue fleece. The word 'tup' – or 'tip' – is used by farmers in some parts of the county to mean ram. Each tup can be put to fifty or sixty

ewes while they're in season. Any ewes that haven't conceived will come back into season after seventeen days and can be mated with a different tup. Ewes which still haven't conceived will come into season for a third time after a further seventeen days. However, Will says they endeavour to have all their ewes in lamb after thirty-four days because that will mean lambing will take place over a more concentrated period the following spring. The breeding process has to be managed because if left to follow their natural instincts, the tups would mate with as many ewes as possible and use up all their reserves. 'The energy involved in mating with 50 or 60 females and fighting off all the other males that are wanting to come and mate with your harem is very sapping,' says Will. 'Some of them would just literally mate themselves to death.' Tups appear to lead quite a pampered existence and aren't sent to the high fells for the winter with the ewes. 'Being a tup is quite good because you do nothing from the middle of December to the middle of November – you just hang around talking to each other and having a smoke,' jokes Will. 'From November onwards you get to mate with all these females; from December to April you're looked after like royalty. They stop on the lowland pasture; they might go to the fell in summer but they wouldn't go back for the winter.'

The ewes are expected to be much tougher. Once they're in lamb they're returned to the fells for the winter and probably won't get any supplementary feed until the last few weeks of their pregnancies. Their gestation period is five months, which means they're brought down for lambing in the first or second week of April. It may seem a harsh way of life, especially compared to the pampered tups but the point of the Herdwick breed is that the animals can exist in hostile conditions. 'Most of them won't receive any feed,' says Will. 'We check on them not that often. The whole point of having them is the fact they're so self-reliant and capable.' When they're born the lambs are jet black, possibly with a little white on their ears. Over time, the wool on their head and legs turns white and their fleeces turn from black to slatey-blue. During springtime, Herdwick fans can keep an eye out for lambs with good prospects: 'One that's going to develop into a good sheep would have a white tinge to its ears or snow white ears,' says Will. After lambing, the ewes stay on the

Herdwick tups – on show at Wasdale – enjoy a more pampered existence than the ewes

*If left to their own devices Herdwick tups would mate with as many ewes
as possible, using up their reserves and jeopardising their survival*

lowlands until their lambs are about 3 weeks old. The lambs are then given marks on their fleeces and ear notches, to identify their home farm, before going up to the fells with their mothers to gain the important hefting instinct. In early to mid-July the mothers and lambs will be brought down again for shearing and for treatment to protect them against parasites, such as sheep ticks. They're back on the fells again until the end of September, when they're brought down and the lambs are weaned, effectively beginning the time when they must fend for themselves. Castrated male lambs are then sold on to be fattened, or fattened on their own farms, ready to enter the food chain. Older ewes, whose teeth are becoming worn, will be sold to lowland farmers. The other ewes are sent back to the fells while their weaned lambs are transported to lower ground farms for the winter, where they benefit from good-quality grass to help them develop. They are already tough enough to return to the fells but by sending them away, farmers free up the grass for the ewes prior to mating. By the time spring comes, the year-old lambs – which are to be the breeding stock of the future – are able to go back to the fells on their own before their mothers join them in May and June after lambing.

Not everyone agrees that upland sheep farming is good for the environment and one newspaper columnist sparked debate when he wrote that Britain's uplands had been 'sheepwrecked' and damaged by over-grazing. Will Rawling and his colleagues believe that it's the sheep that have created the Lake District landscape which visitors come to admire: 'Some people would argue they're doing the opposite and wrecking the fells,' says Will. 'But as sheep flocks reduce, we're seeing an increase in bracken and there's more juniper. I would say the fells would be less accessible without Herdwicks – you would be looking at a different type of fell. The stone walls would probably fall into disrepair and farmsteads would be converted into holiday homes. It would cease to be a working environment.' Will agrees that the fells should be available for everyone but hopes that people bear in mind that they're part of the rural economy as well as the landscape. 'I think people have to remember that the fells are part of an active working, farming system. As sheep farmers we're really pleased people come out and enjoy them. We would hope that would continue and people would go out there and enjoy the fells however and when they like, as long as they do it safely – but much of what they're enjoying has happened as a result of sheep farming.' Will believes the Herdwicks are an integral part of the Lake District: 'The Herdwicks have more to do with the Lake District than the Lake District has to do with Herdwicks. The Herdwicks are very much part of the Lake District. They're an adapted breed: they're the colour they are because of the

Sam Rawling, pictured here, farms with his father, Will, in the Ennerdale Valley; their ancestors began breeding Herdwicks there in 1524

vegetation they eat. The pigment in the wool is a direct result of the herbs they're eating and the colour of the heather comes through in the colour of the wool.'

Will says there is a need to balance grazing with nature but not at the expense of reducing Herdwick numbers below a critical number needed to maintain the breed. After all, if the hefting structure is lost, it's gone forever. A change in the way farm subsidies are allocated, away from a system based on stock levels and towards environmental schemes, often requires farmers to reduce their stock numbers. 'Once we get below a certain critical mass it's really quite difficult to maintain the diverse genetics that we need and to provide surplus stock for the farmer to sell off as produce and stock,' says Will. Like their animals, Herdwick sheep farmers are tough but they would welcome the opportunity to have their say in how farming should develop. As Will puts it: 'Herdwick farmers are very resilient people and they will meet every challenge full on and do what they can to continue farming Herdwick sheep.'

Will has great feeling for his sheep but nevertheless farming Herdwicks is how he makes his living:

> I've spent a long time working with Herdwick sheep and I have a great sentimental attachment to Herdwick sheep but I'm also a businessman and if Herdwick sheep weren't providing me with what I consider to be a worthwhile farming operation I wouldn't have Herdwicks, I would have something different. Herdwick sheep are very much a commercial farming option. They've evolved and developed into the sheep best suited to the systems that we can operate in the Lake District.

Will says that the tough animals contribute so much to the Lake District and actually give farmers four products: meat; wool; environmental and habitat management; and heritage and culture. After all, as Will says: 'Tourists come to see what Herdwicks have created.'

Farmers mark their Herdwicks with different colours to identify them on the fells

CHAPTER 3

THE SCAFELLS

THE SUMMER OF 2013 was warm and dry and as a consequence, the summit of England's highest mountain sometimes resembled a metropolitan park on a lazy Sunday afternoon. Groups of people could be found sitting about the rocky landscape, eating packed lunches, taking photographs, batting away annoying midges and using their mobile phones, as they congratulated themselves on having climbed the 978m or 3,210ft to the top of Scafell Pike.

By August of that year, it was calculated that at least 80,000 people had used the main Brown Tongue route from Wasdale to reach the summit but others would also have made the climb using alternative approaches. Many were charity walkers who were being sponsored to complete a Three Peaks event, by climbing Scafell Pike and Britain's other two tallest peaks, Ben Nevis in Scotland and Snowdon in Wales. These challenges are often attempted within a twenty-four-hour period. In reaching the roof of England, the adventure seekers were following a long tradition that began in earnest after 1860, when the first Ordnance Survey confirmed this was the highest point in the Scafell massif – a group of mountains which had previously been known as the Pikes of Scafell. Dorothy Wordsworth, the poet's sister, climbed to the top of Scafell Pike in October 1818 with her friend, Miss Barker. In a letter, Dorothy described how they were initially hoping to climb Scafell – Scafell Pike's sister mountain which is just 14m shorter – but they found that even after they had slogged to the beginning of the climb, the ascent would have been 'exceedingly steep and difficult, so that we might have been benighted if we had attempted it'. They decided to climb Scafell Pike instead. William Wordsworth used Dorothy's account in a later edition of his hugely successful *Guide to the Lakes*, which included the passage: 'On the summit of the Pike, which we gained after much toil, though without difficulty, there was not a breath of air to stir even the papers containing our refreshment, as they lay spread out upon a rock.' In this description, Dorothy was summoning up a scene that would have been familiar to those climbing the peak in 2013. The *Guide* continues: 'But the majesty of the mountains below, and close to us, is not to be conceived.' That sense of awe and wonder was also felt by many of those who made it to the top 200 years after Dorothy.

It's not known if Wordsworth himself ever reached Scafell Pike's summit but Simon Bainbridge, Professor of Romantic Studies at Lancaster University, says that he would have used his sister's description of the climb – and another of a visit that she made to Ullswater – in his *Guide to the Lakes* because he thought they were well written, not just because he didn't have his own experiences to fall back on. 'So Wordsworth certainly used Dorothy's account. My sense would be this was not so much because he needed an account of an excursion to Scafell – these are the only excursions he includes, after all, so they wouldn't be missed if they weren't there – but rather that he admired Dorothy's accounts of the excursions and thought they would be a valuable addition to the volume.' Defeated by Scafell but able to climb its taller neighbour, Scafell Pike, without difficulty, Dorothy also inadvertently highlighted the different characteristics of the mountains and the feelings that they continue to inspire. Many believe that although Scafell Pike is the higher mountain, Scafell is the peak with all the grandeur. Scafell is also the mountain most admired by climbers for

Before it was confirmed as the highest point in England in 1860, Scafell Pike, on the left, was thought by some to be smaller than its sister mountain, Scafell, seen on the right

its challenges. Alfred Wainwright, the great guidebook author, identified this himself in Book Four of his series *A Pictorial Guide to the Lakeland Fells*. He explained that when the mountains were first named, the whole massif was known as Scaw Fell. Later on, people used that name to apply to the mountain which seemed tallest – which was Scafell, as it's now spelled. The other summits were known collectively as the Pikes of Scaw Fell. Wainwright wrote that even when it was discovered that Scafell Pike was the highest peak in the group and therefore in England, many people maintained that Scafell was the superior mountain.

Bill Birkett, who has spent a lifetime visiting, climbing, writing about and photographing the Scafell massif, can relate to that point of view. Scafell, he says, offers much more to climbers than its taller sister and being on the mountain is much more challenging than simply slogging up Scafell Pike: 'It's much more of a climbers' mountain than Scafell Pike. In the early days Scafell looks like the highest mountain so it's not until the first survey that they realise that Scafell Pike is actually a bit higher. Before that the Victorian climbers would go to Scafell.' A successful climber, Bill has become best known for his mountain writing and photography. The Scafell massif has played a large part in his life and he wrote a book about the range of peaks, which was published in 2007. The massif is a huge, jagged plateau from which rise the peaks of Great End, Broad Crag, Ill Crag, Scafell Pike and Scafell. The summit of Scafell Pike is covered with some of the roughest boulders in the Lake District and the footpath which leads to it is marked by many cairns. The north and east flanks of Scafell have distinct characteristics: Central Buttress is a huge bastion of rock and East Buttress is an improbable barrel-shaped overhanging crag. The fissure known as Broad Stand finds a weakness from Mickledore ridge between the two flanks. To the west, the massif falls away to grass. Bill's first experience of Scafell was as a young boy accompanying his father, Jim Birkett, on walks. Jim was one of the most talented and famous rock climbers of his generation, dominating the sport from the 1930s until the '50s. He was also a naturalist, interested in birds and plants. Bill's early trips with Jim were to look for rare plants on Cam Spout, which is on Scafell in Eskdale. 'I remember those trips always being the

Scafell Pike, England's highest peak, is a rock-strewn plateau

favourite outings on the fells, to Scafell with my dad.' At first, his view of the Scafell range wasn't to do with it as a place to climb: 'It's funny because I suppose I thought about it in different terms: either rich with plants or interesting with peregrine falcons nesting and that was the kind of take on it I experienced as a kid.' Eventually, Jim also told him about its significance as a place to climb, although he didn't point out his own achievements on the mountain. 'I always remember my dad pointing out the East Buttress of Scafell. He said, "That's the most forbidding mountain crag in Britain." I remember looking at it in some kind of awe and thinking, "Yeah."'

His father's description must have had an impact as Bill first went to climb the mountain when he was about 15. He and some friends set off from Seathwaite with ropes, a tent and big rucksacks to make camp. The weather turned out to be appalling but on the first evening conditions were ideal as they approached the East Buttress of Scafell, one of its two main faces:

It was an absolutely perfect evening, sunny and warm. We did the classic route, Great Eastern. Dad had told me about it and said it was fantastically exposed and a great route. That night we absolutely romped up it; it seemed like a walk, like a stroll in the park as these things are when you're a kid and you're really fired up. We thought the world's our oyster if we can do this.

But that was to be as good as it got on that trip: 'The next day we got up and it was absolutely throwing it down.' After such an auspicious start, it was no surprise that Bill became enchanted with the massif, which came to play a significant part in his climbing life and his writing and photography career. As a climber, Bill claimed some first ascents – or first-recorded climbs of a route – on Scafell. His favourite crag on the massif and in the whole Lake District is Esk Buttress, known as Dow Crag, which he describes as a huge sweep of volcanic rock. 'It's a big pillar of rock, which is just a stunning climb, really aesthetic, really challenging. Esk Buttress is my favourite crag in the Lake District. It's just fantastic; you look down over that great mass and it feels like you're in a different world.' Bill also had a big fall on Scafell Crag when he was still a teenager and he remembers 'falling through space'. It was a reminder that Scafell is a potentially dangerous group of mountains: 'It made me think a bit. It made me realise I wasn't immortal and gravity was a definite thing I had to be aware of.'

After the warm and largely dry summer of 2013, when so many walkers and Three Peaks challengers flocked to Scafell Pike, some of the problems associated with large-scale use of the Lake District fells came to a head. Footpath erosion, a concern on the fells for several decades, was much discussed. It was announced that £250,000 was needed to combat erosion and for widening and maintenance of Brown Tongue, the main route to Scafell from Wasdale. There were other issues also aired by people living and working in the Wasdale Valley about the Three Peakers and what were felt to be inadequate facilities. Litter spilled out of bins and it was said that some walkers were even leaving human waste behind them on the mountain. The lack of preparation by a number of walkers, some of whom didn't carry a map, was also proving alarming

for local people. It wasn't unusual for a walker to set off from Borrowdale, summit Scafell Pike and then lose his or her way coming down and arrive in Wasdale by mistake, facing a long walk or expensive taxi ride to meet his companions or pick up his lift. A tale was told of a climber who didn't even know from which valley he had set out – a helpful local worked it out from his description. One local resident, arriving in the morning to open her business premises, had to avoid running over exhausted walkers lying in the road. The problems were said to be exacerbated because Scafell Pike is located between Ben Nevis and Snowdon, so it's always tackled second by Three Peakers, who are either making their way north or south. This means that the climbers often arrive in the Lake District in the early hours of the morning, when they are beginning to flag and when most disturbance is likely to be caused. Certainly the voluntary members of the local mountain rescue team were feeling over-stretched that summer. Three Peaks walkers who called them because it was dark and they were lost but who weren't in danger or other difficulties found that the team wouldn't turn out to guide them down, leaving them instead to find their own way after dawn. The rescuers' group leaders said that it was better that they weren't turning out in the middle of the night but were instead fresh for the next call out, which could be to a heart attack victim. The organisers of long-standing Three Peak challenges defended themselves and said they went to great lengths to ensure the walks went ahead safely. It was often independent people who got themselves into difficulty and gained Three Peakers a bad reputation, they said. Local people were hopeful that Three Peakers would make a contribution to footpath repair funds, helping to put right some of the damage done by everyone who uses the mountain. Bill Birkett isn't a fan of the crowds who flog up Scafell Pike but he's wary of laying down the law on Scafell and in other wild places: 'I do believe that mountains provide great freedom and that shouldn't be interfered with. Once you start making too many rules and regulations it detracts even further from these special places.'

One of the most famous accounts of climbing on Scafell was given by Samuel Taylor Coleridge, Wordsworth's friend and fellow poet. In August 1802 he made a Lakeland tour that included a now-famous descent from

➤ *Many climbers regard Central Buttress on Scafell, right, as more challenging than its higher sister mountain, Scafell Pike, seen on the left*

▼ *While Scafell Pike can often be thronged with Three Peak challengers, Scafell, at just 14m shorter, is likely to be deserted*

▲ *The summit of Scafell Pike has become a magnet for walkers attempting Britain's three highest peaks, sometimes causing disruption for local people*

▼ *The description of Samuel Taylor Coleridge's perilous descent through Broad Stand, seen here above Mickledore ridge, became one of the most famous accounts of early rock climbing*

Scafell through what's called Broad Stand. In his book, Bill Birkett calls it a 'mind-blowing descent' of the series of rocky steps and corners. Certainly what Coleridge achieved was remarkable, even applying today's standards. His method of climbing down – simply by dropping to the next ledge – was incredibly risky because he had no knowledge of what was ahead of him. Coleridge wrote in a letter that one of the drops was twice his own height and on to a narrow ledge. He was in danger, he wrote, of falling backwards and perishing. In the letter he writes of how frightened he was and overawed by the sight of the crags and the clouds, so that he found himself in a type of trance. In his book, Bill Birkett explains that today rock climbers use Broad Stand as a route down between the crags, although most runners and walkers wouldn't want to tackle it without a rope. It was an audacious scramble and Bill regards Coleridge's account of it as a gripping passage of mountain literature. Bill says: 'Shepherds must have used that route long before that recorded descent of Coleridge but that was the first written account of it. It's a very powerful piece of writing.' Coleridge has since been identified as one of the pioneers of mountaineering as a pastime; something to be attempted for enjoyment rather than economic necessity.

There's no doubt that walkers and Three Peakers will continue to hike up Scafell Pike, eschewing the delights to be found in exploring Scafell. 'That's absolutely right and let's hope they keep off it,' jokes Bill Birkett. In reality, however, he enjoys telling people about what the Scafell range means to him and why it's worth spending time on the mountain. 'It's obviously been hugely significant really, to write a book about it – a book about a single mountain massif.' Scafell has many different facets and faces, unlike Ben Nevis for example, which is a summit on its own. 'It's one range of mountains but it's very varied and interesting,' says Bill. 'Every time I go I discover something new.' Dorothy Wordsworth grasped the beauty of Scafell Pike during her ascent of 1818, writing: 'No gems or flowers can surpass in colouring the beauty of some of these masses of stone …' If she returned today she would find the beauty of the stones unchanged, despite thousands of feet over many decades having pounded their way to the roof of England.

Efforts are being made to repair damage caused by thousands of pairs of walkers' boots as they trek from Wasdale to the summit of Scafell Pike

CHAPTER 4

TODAY'S LITERARY LIONS
Hunter Davies and Melvyn Bragg

IN 1787, a young man left his grammar school in Cumbria and went to study at university. He travelled in Europe and lived in the south of England but found himself drawn back to the place of his birth, eventually returning to live in the Lake District. Uniquely talented, he made his living through his writing and came to be regarded as one of our greatest poets. His poetry encompassed many themes but the landscape of Cumbria and the Lake District continued to exert a major influence over his work.

Almost two centuries after William Wordsworth went up to Cambridge, two young men, both born in the 1930s, left their grammar schools in Cumbria to study at university. They also used their talent with words to make their livings. Both wrote fiction and non-fiction. One became a noted biographer, a Fleet Street journalist and long-standing newspaper columnist, the other a famous broadcaster and cultural commentator, author and life peer.

Living in London in the 1960s, both were soon immersed in the culture of the period. Urbane and urban-dwelling, these were no country hicks down from an obscure rural backwater. Television, the Beatles, football and radio were on their radars. Despite this, like Wordsworth before them, both felt the pull of their home county and regularly headed back to Cumbria. Today they're in demand for their cultural savvy and work keeps them in London but they both still spend part of the year in the Lakes.

The Lake District has long been and continues to be associated with writers. Wordsworth, Samuel Taylor Coleridge, Robert Southey, John Ruskin, Beatrix Potter, Hugh Walpole and Arthur Ransome are among those who've found solace in the Lakeland landscape and taken inspiration from their surroundings. Hunter Davies and Melvyn Bragg, the two Cumbrian lads who have never abandoned their home county, continue that literary heritage. The Lake District has figured in their work: Hunter Davies wrote biographies of Wordsworth and the Lake District fell walker Alfred Wainwright as well as guides of his own. Cumbria, meanwhile, has loomed large in Melvyn Bragg's fiction. He says he feels uniquely relaxed when he's back in the area where he was raised.

Hunter and his wife, the novelist Margaret Forster, spend about half the year in Cumbria and half in London. They both grew up in Carlisle and Hunter says they've spent a lifetime exploring the countryside around their homes: 'When we were courting we used to come hostelling in the Lakes.' Hunter identifies a split in their year: they have an urban life and a rural life within a twelve-month period with two sets of friends and two sets of activities. But wherever he is, he works on his books and his newspaper columns in the same way: 'People think you need to live in pretty places to be inspired in your writing. That's not true. It inspires you as a person and makes you happy and you love it but it doesn't make you a writer, good or bad.' But when he's away from the capital, it doesn't exert the same pull on him that Cumbria does. The Lake District has a unique place in his affections: 'I don't pine for London except for the children and grandchildren but in London, we pine for here.'

When Hunter and Margaret first returned to Cumbria it was to see their parents and to bring the children for school holidays. 'But we always said when the last of the children leaves home – which they never do these days – we'll look for something in the Lakes proper. We wanted

Hunter Davies spends each summer in his native Cumbria, swimming in Crummock Water as often as the weather permits

Hunter Davies loves the variety of Lake District landscapes – which have featured in several of his books – and finds it draws him back each year

to be on a lake, or as near a lake as possible.' In the event, they found a house in Loweswater village within striking distance of three lakes. Their nearest is Crummock Water and they can also walk to Loweswater and Buttermere. Hunter keeps a record of the number of days when it's warm enough for him to swim in Crummock Water; ideally it would be every day. Our interview is conducted outdoors in the sunshine and Hunter agrees to pose in the lake for photographs, using the opportunity to have his second swim of the day. He's nut-brown from hours spent outside and he clearly knows the area around the lake, stopping to chat to some neighbours. The issue of second-home owners can be contentious in Cumbrian communities but Hunter points out that family members occupy the house when he and Margaret are in London.

Hunter is best known for his biography of the Beatles, published in 1968, which remains the only authorised biography of the group. He's helped to write autobiographies for the footballers Paul Gascoigne and Wayne Rooney and the politician John Prescott. His book *The Glory Game*, published in 1972, was one of the first books to examine the phenomenon of the professional football team and is regarded as a classic of its genre. His columns include a long-running slot in *The Sunday Times*. The author of forty books plus children's titles, he's still called on to comment on contemporary culture: for example, his expertise on Beatlemania is sought when hysteria surrounding the latest boy band is compared to the reception of the Fab Four in their heyday. He was back in the headlines recently when he donated his collection of John Lennon letters and lyrics to the British Museum.

But he's never escaped his Lakeland literary heritage and he's mined Cumbria's people and places as rich seams for his work. He says he wasn't conscious of those Lake District writers who had gone before him while he was growing up but once he'd begun to write himself, they became part of his inheritance. One book about Cumbria led on to another: while he was researching a book about his home county, *A Walk Around the Lakes*, he found out more about Wordsworth. 'I read all the stuff on Wordsworth I could find and the standard biography was two volumes, which I found unreadable. There wasn't one general biography for the normally educated man in the pub, that's why I did that biography.' He also tackled the life story of the fell walker Alfred Wainwright. He'd once spent three hours with Wainwright and afterwards met the author's wife, Betty. She had been hanging some of her husband's drawings for an exhibition and Hunter asked if he could buy three for his own collection. When he went to write the cheque, he inadvertently became one of the first people to discover that Wainwright was giving his not insubstantial earnings to an animal charity.

Wordsworth didn't want tourists to flood into the area, although his best-selling book was his *Guide to the Lakes*. But Hunter believes the Lake District should be open to everyone. Fears about tourists swamping Cumbria have proved unfounded, he says. Not only have the numbers of visitors remained quite stable but the environment is being better protected now than ever before, with work being carried out to prevent footpath erosion: 'The final thing is it belongs to everybody; it doesn't belong to people who live here.' Just as Peter Mayle was criticised in the 1990s when his books about Provence sent tourists flocking to France to discover his idyll for themselves, Hunter has found himself admonished for encouraging people to visit Cumbria. It's the one negative he puts forward about his home county: 'The only thing that annoys me is the locals saying "You're ruining it by writing about it." Also the people that get in, the offcomers – which I like to think I'm not – they want to draw up the drawbridge because they're in.' There's hardly anything that he doesn't like about the Lake District. Even the food has improved. Whereas fifty years ago there was nowhere decent to eat, the pubs today – such as his local, the Kirkstile Inn – serve fantastic meals. The Lake District has everything in a relatively small area: 'You can go from massive frightening crags in half an hour to Beatrix Potter nursery-type landscapes.' One day, he says he and Margaret will be 'too decrepit' to continue living in their rural idyll and then they'll be forced to leave it permanently and head to London. But until then, the Lakes will continue to draw him home to Cumbria: 'The Lake District is the big attraction: it's so stunning and wonderful and there's so much here. Even if it hadn't been home I think I would have liked to have a second cottage here.'

Melvyn Bragg, now Lord Bragg, spends much of his time in London but knows he can be back in Cumbria whenever he wants. He's owned the house he shares with his wife, the writer Cate Haste, on the edge of the northern fells, for more than forty years. 'I don't have to pine, I can just jump on a train,' is his practical solution to being homesick. 'Cumbria's still my emotional centre but the fact is my family's based in London, my children were born in London, although they've come here (Cumbria) an awful lot, every year of their lives.' He's relaxed in his home and is happy to be interviewed dressed down in a waistcoat that was a gift from his daughter. Running his hands through his instantly recognisable full head of thick, wavy hair as he speaks, he pauses before he answers, searching for the words which best articulate his views. Growing up in the north Cumbrian town of Wigton, he used to bike to the Lakes and visit Keswick, or take a boat out on Bassenthwaite. When he first left Cumbria for Oxford, where he went to university, he didn't want to quit his home town: 'I thought Wigton was great; I'd got my friends there, got my girlfriend there, there wasn't much else that I wanted. For the first year I didn't think Oxford was anything like as interesting as Wigton. Then I got used to it.' When he was able to, he rented a cottage for his visits home: 'As soon as I could afford to come back, I came back.'

Melvyn is known as the long-standing presenter of ITV's flagship arts programme *The South Bank Show* – now broadcast on Sky Arts HD – and has come to be regarded as an authority on contemporary culture. He is chancellor of the University of Leeds and was appointed to the House of Lords as a Labour life peer. His wide-ranging non-fiction work has encompassed the history of language, the King James Bible and a biography of Richard Burton. Notwithstanding his metropolitan interests, his fiction has returned to his native landscape and two trilogies follow the fortunes of ordinary Cumbrian families. His first novel, called *Mirrors and Wire*, which was never published despite interest from Faber and Faber, was partly set in Carlisle. 'I've just never really gone away,' he says. 'When I started to write fiction, when I was about 18 or 19, the first story I wrote was set up here; a lot of my fiction has been set up here.' He was aware of his home county's literary heritage: 'If you grow up in

this county and you are decent at English ...' He breaks off to indicate his book-lined study: 'You don't know how many volumes of Wordsworth I got as school prizes – most of them are in there.' Coming from Cumbria meant that the looming figure and inheritance of Cumbria's Poet Laureate had to be addressed: 'You've got to make a decision: are you going to rip this up or are you going to take him on board as the key man?'

Melvyn says he decided to take Wordsworth on board. Initially he thought the poet's shorter work compared unfavourably with that of John Keats but once he'd read Wordsworth's great autobiographical poem, *The Prelude*, he grew to admire him more and more. Knowing that Wordsworth, Thomas Hardy, D.H. Lawrence and Leo Tolstoy wrote about the landscapes that they knew reassured him that he could do the same. But he acknowledges that for a child growing up, his world is the world that he knows and loves. Just as he loved Wigton, Liverpool would have been 'the whole world' for the young Paul McCartney. Although he'd grown up in a relatively remote town, he didn't notice anyone patronising him when he went up to Oxford because of his northern roots. 'If I did, I didn't have anything to do with them.' His attitude would have been, he says: 'They can bugger off.' In fact, he says he was part of a group of young people who were given tremendous opportunities to make their marks on radio and television in the 1960s.

These days, when he's in Cumbria, Melvyn catches up with friends and family. He enjoys walking and likes to climb a nearby hill. 'Binsey's our little fell; there's a wonderful view right down into the Lakes. On a good day you can see the sea and see the Isle of Man.' There is a route up the back of Skiddaw mountain – one of the highest in the lakes – which he enjoys walking and Derwentwater is his favourite lake. 'These northern fells are where I feel most comfortable; I like the emptiness of them. You can walk a long time without seeing anybody. It's a bit selfish but it's nice.' The Lake District is also a land of contrasts: the large lakes of Windermere and Ullswater remind him of Switzerland. Melvyn thinks the organisations tasked with looking after the landscape have done a good job of protecting the environment. Sometimes they can be overzealous: a zip wire attraction proposed for Honister was rejected as unsuitable for

*Melvyn Bragg feels uniquely relaxed
when he's back in his home county*

the landscape, even though a similar set up had been used historically to transport slate off the mountainside. 'Sometimes they can go too far. I think that zip wire would be fun for a lot of kids and it's an area where there have been zip wires for about 100 years.'

Like Hunter, he doesn't need to be in the Lake District to find inspiration and works in the same way whether he's in London or Cumbria: 'The great thing when you're a writer is it's easy to sit down with a bit of paper and get on with it.' But he recognises that the Cumbrian landscape has an impact on people's minds. Like many before him, Melvyn finds the Lake District improves his well-being: 'Just being here makes me feel relaxed. I just feel I can go out the door and go up Binsey and go down to Derwentwater or into the Lakes and it's fine. It definitely has a calming effect. I like walking through London but there's nothing like up here.'

Now Lord Bragg, the teenage Melvyn was at first reluctant to leave his home town of Wigton for university at Oxford. He has become known as a novelist and non-fiction writer, a broadcaster and cultural commentator

CHAPTER 5

ALFRED WAINWRIGHT

I N JUNE 1930, two young men visited the Lake District for the first time, travelling by bus from Blackburn in Lancashire and arriving at Windermere. They went straight to climb Orrest Head, a 239m or 784ft hill that can be reached easily and quickly from the town. The hill itself isn't remarkable but the view from the top is: a wide vista of England's largest lake opens up and behind Windermere are some of the Lake District's most magnificent high peaks, including Scafell Pike, Great End and the group of mountains known as the Langdale Pikes. The two men were 23-year-old Alfred Wainwright and his cousin, Eric Beardsall. There was nothing particularly notable about their trip but it was a holiday that was to change the course of Alfred's life and arguably the cultural history of the Lake District.

Wainwright, or A.W. as he was often known, went on to become the most famous guidebook author of all time, read and admired throughout the world and attracting a group of dedicated fans and followers. Self-published at first, his seven *Pictorial Guide to the Lakeland Fells*, published from 1955 to 1966, became best-sellers, largely through word of mouth, and are regarded by many walkers as never having been bettered. Printed and reproduced exactly as A.W. wrote and drew them, with detailed sketches and perfect handwriting, the books are talked of by their fans as works of art. The 214 peaks which he writes about in the *Pictorial Guide* series have become known as 'the Wainwrights' and fans and followers still attempt to climb them all, in order to join the club of those who've completed the challenge. In a similar way to Beatrix Potter, A.W. was an offcomer who discovered the Lake District, fell in love with the landscape, moved to the

area, wrote books which are still in print and popular all over the world and in the process became inextricably linked with the Lake District and part of its cultural history. He wrote more than sixty titles in all and became a television star in later life. When he died in 1991 he was eulogised and praised, with tributes in the national press. Eric Robson, who is chairman of The Wainwright Society, knew him well and was the journalist who appeared with him on his first television programmes in the '80s. He says A.W. achieved a rare feat: 'I frequently compared him with the man who designed the London Underground map. He pulled off a similar trick, that he took a three-dimensional object – in Wainwright's case a Lakeland mountain – and made it into a two-dimensional image and made it more understandable. That shouldn't work and yet it does, very definitely. If you look at the very best pictorial image of the Lake District, the very best photographic books of the Lakeland mountains, they don't make the mountains as understandable as Wainwright's pen and ink drawings.'

Back in 1930, all that was still to come but it could be argued that A.W.'s course was set as soon as he reached the top of Orrest Head. He was later to write how seeing the view open up before him was 'a moment of magic' and that he stood transfixed, unable to believe his eyes. He saw mountain ranges, rich woodlands, pastures and the shimmering lake. He recognised the Langdale Pikes from photographs and wrote that they looked 'exciting and friendly'. Perhaps most significantly of all, A.W. fancied they were beckoning to him: 'Come on and join us, they seemed to say.' Eric Robson explains why the view would have had quite the impact on the young Alfred that it did:

Innominate Tarn: Wainwright's ashes were scattered on its shores

Wainwright's first glimpse of the Lake District: the view from Orrest Head across Windermere to the Langdale Pikes

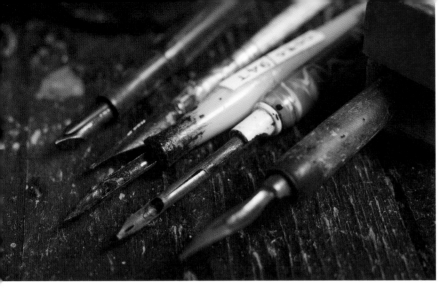

▲ *A.W. wrote and drew his* Pictorial Guide *series by hand (personal possessions of A.W. photographed by kind permission of Kendal Museum and the Wainwright Estate)*

▼ *In self-portraits in his* Pictorial Guide *series, A.W. would often be depicted with his pipe*

You've got to remember the context – that he had come from a world that was hemmed in by mill chimneys and walls. He's been exploring the hills around Blackburn, he would go up to Darwen Tower but wherever you look from Darwen Tower you see the remains of industry and so it was a revelation to him, being able to look out from Orrest Head and not see a single factory. He had a pretty hard upbringing, he came from the school of hard knocks and poverty and the fact was that he had to work his socks off because he knew the only way of getting out of that was to work his way out of it.

A.W. was born in Blackburn. His father, a stonemason by trade, was an alcoholic and his caring mother struggled to feed her family of four children. A bright boy, A.W. did well at school and in 1920, the year he turned 13, he secured a sought-after job at Blackburn Town Hall. He had to study for another ten years to pass his professional accountancy exams. However, Eric says he approached his studies and his job with a light heart and that, as a young man, there was a vibrancy about him of which people aren't aware. Eric is fascinated by the younger Wainwright, who is most apparent in the book *A Pennine Journey*, written in 1938 but not published until 1986, after he had become an established author. This was a young man who perfectly captured workmates and bosses in his cartoons and who had a strong sense of fun. A popular image of Wainwright is as a grumpy older gentleman, with a shock of white hair and whiskers. Eric says:

I feel rather guilty about it, because quite a lot of the image of Wainwright as the curmudgeonly old duffer was brought about by me, because he was an old man by the time Richard Else, the producer, persuaded him to make the programme, so the main image people have in their mind's eye is of an old bewhiskered chap.

People who knew Wainwright – and many who didn't – have a view of him as someone who didn't like people. His apparent grumpiness and his decision to leave the money he made from his books to animal charities helped to foster that view. But Eric defends him:

People are forever telling me what Wainwright thought and I need to make it clear, I'm not Wainwright on earth but yes I did know him well and I liked him and liked his company very much and he was not anywhere near the curmudgeonly old sod that opinion would let us believe. He had a very well-honed sense of humour, Saharan dry and a lot of people misread him because his aim was so sharp.

The idea that A.W. didn't like people is also challenged by Hunter Davies in his biography of the author. Hunter points out that A.W. was capable of great kindness and generosity but almost always preferred to interact with people by letter, rather than in person. Throughout his life he would have perhaps twenty correspondences on the go but face-to-face encounters appeared to alarm him. Eric says that, in common with other people who deal with complex ideas on different levels and across different disciplines, A.W. was prone to changing his mind, so that expressing an opinion about what he would have wanted – for example about a suggestion to posthumously put up a statue of him in Kendal – becomes problematic.

Following the first trip to Orrest Head in 1930, Wainwright visited the Lake District many times and finally moved permanently to the area in 1941, leaving his job in Blackburn to take up a post as accountancy assistant at Kendal Town Hall. He was promoted to borough treasurer in 1948, at the age of 41. He began writing the first of his *Pictorial Guide* series a few years after his move, carrying out his research on trips into the Lake District. A non-driver, he had to rely on the bus service or on lifts from friends. He became a prolific author later in life and produced books about other areas: the Pennines, the Highlands of Scotland, the coast-to-coast route from St Bees Head to Robin Hood's Bay, the Dales and parts of Wales. But for many people, the seven original *Pictorial Guide to the Lakeland Fells* books have a magical quality to them. If he had decided, on that June day in 1930, to travel into the Peak District instead of the Lake District, the question arises whether he would have embarked on such a project as the *Pictorial Guide* series and if he had, whether he would have been as successful. Eric believes that while we

Wainwright's rucksack, walking boots, much-darned socks, pipe, tobacco and pens and ink

A frozen Innominate Tarn with Great Gable in the background

can never know for sure and Wainwright wrote well about Yorkshire's limestone country and the Howgills, there was and is something about the Lake District that brought out A.W.'s best qualities:

> His talent and the finest upland landscape in England combined make it a powerful achievement. It has the greatest variety of any landscape in England: from the rugged harshness of the Wasdale Valley to the gentler wilderness of Borrowdale, you're only going about five miles apart and yet you've got these huge contrasts. It was a hell of a canvas to work on and a canvas with more variety and more themes and more theatre than you would get in any landscape in England. I suspect that he wouldn't have become so compulsively drawn to the landscape anywhere else. Every corner he walked round he found something fresh and something new in the Lake District.

Great as they are, the landscapes of the Yorkshire Dales and Brecon Beacons wouldn't have provided him with as much material. A.W.'s stepdaughter, Jane King, says there was something about the Lake District and its mountains which was especially alluring for the author: 'He thought the Lakes was so amazingly beautiful.'

Discussion of A.W. often focuses on his private life: his unhappy first marriage to Ruth Holden; his second, very happy marriage to Betty McNally; the fact that he left his money to animal welfare and nothing at all to his only child, Peter. Eric says that A.W. wasn't blind to his own faults:

> He himself had many regrets about his first marriage and the way he treated Ruth. He didn't pull any punches about himself. I think he stands up to scrutiny. He owns up to the fact he wasn't a perfect chap, certainly not a perfect husband the first time round. At the end of his life he found immense happiness with Betty, they were a marvellous couple.

Betty was often the one to drive him to spots from where he could start his walks but even after marriage to his sweetheart it seems old habits died hard: 'He joked that he only married her because she had a driver's licence and she still had to walk fifteen paces behind him when they went on their expeditions on the hills because he liked the experience of isolation.'

But although his professional and serious exterior hid a far more romantic and passionate personality than most people could have guessed, it's what A.W. achieved on paper and his relationship with the Lake District which continues to fascinate his followers and fans. In 2002, The Wainwright Society was formed, 'to keep alive the things which A.W. promoted through the guidebooks'. Its members have also raised thousands of pounds for good causes, following A.W.'s example. The mountaineers Sir Chris Bonington and Doug Scott, the television presenter Julia Bradbury and the journalist and author Stuart Maconie are among those who have become members. Eric Robson has been the society's chairman since its inception. He says it was at the urging of A.W.'s widow, Betty, who was concerned about ideas being floated to commemorate the author, such as putting up plaques on the fells. In accordance with his wishes, A.W.'s ashes had been scattered by the side of Innominate Tarn on Haystacks and there was even a proposal, Eric says, to change the name of the tarn in honour of A.W. 'I was on a three-line whip from Betty to stand as chairman so I could keep the worst excesses at bay.' Eric says that he's proud that more than ten years on, the only plaque is in Buttermere church, which is set in a window from where there is a view of Haystacks. The wording encourages the visitor to pause and remember A.W. and to lift their eyes to Haystacks, his favourite place.

There is little doubt about the impact that the Lake District had on A.W. Eric says that A.W. also had a considerable effect on his adopted home, encouraging walkers to visit the area. The chairman of visitor body Cumbria Tourism, Eric remembers a survey which was conducted to gauge the impact of a Hollywood film about Beatrix Potter, starring Renée Zellweger. Among the questions, visitors were asked what had influenced them to come to the Lake District. About 7 per cent of people mentioned Miss Potter and 17 per cent said Alfred Wainwright. A.W.'s stepdaughter, Jane King, says that when people find out about her connection to the author, they fall into one of two groups: either they know nothing about

him or they're passionate about his books and work. 'It's very interesting how people sometimes you would not have expected turn out to be really, really interested and have A.W. books.' The Wainwright Society, of which Jane and her sister, Annie Sellar, are joint presidents, holds a memorial lecture every year featuring a prominent speaker. Since A.W.'s death, Eric says the author has been criticised for encouraging too many people to the Lake District and especially 'the wrong sort'. A.W. himself could be sniffy about those who didn't appreciate the landscape or didn't stray far from their cars, expressing views that echo those of fellow guidebook author William Wordsworth, who later expressed horror at the thought of thousands of unsuitable visitors arriving by train. However, Eric thinks the construction of the M6 did more to open up Cumbria to visitors than A.W. If walkers follow the *Pictorial Guide* series and what A.W. recommends, they won't go far wrong, Eric says: 'You won't damage the mountains because his love of the place so shines through his work that you wouldn't dare damage it.' Sales of the *Pictorial Guide* series reached 1 million during his lifetime and his books have continued to sell well. They have been revised once, to take account of changes to the routes and the landscape and a further set of updates may be made, although many fans continue to prefer the originals. The television programmes *Wainwright Walks*, presented by Julia Bradbury, caused another spike in interest when they were broadcast from 2007. It's an incredible achievement for someone who had to self-publish his first book and who was never going to jump through hoops to publicise his work. However, Eric reckons that A.W. knew the value of what he could do and what he'd produced and wouldn't be surprised at the continued interest in his work, even more than twenty years after his death. 'By the time he got the first book published he knew he had something on his hands that was too good to grace just one person's bookshelves. He knew he had struck gold and got a winner.' The idea of an unknown author selling 1 million copies of a non-fiction work largely by word of mouth was remarkable then and remains so. A.W. later said that the first *Pictorial Guide* was originally intended only as a personal chronicle and that the idea of publication came later. But Eric believes there was a certain amount of 'baloney' in the idea they were never destined to be published and were simply an aide-memoire. He remembers taking A.W. out to Haystacks for the last time, when the author's eyesight was failing and the weather was poor. 'It was a misty day with horrendous rain and from the top you couldn't see a damn thing but that was no impediment to Wainwright; he just ticked off the summits that he couldn't see.' He knew exactly what the landscape looked like, in his mind's eye. Eric says: 'He never needed that aide-memoire.'

The only memorial plaque to A.W. in the Lake District is in Buttermere church, where visitors are invited to lift their eyes to Haystacks

A.W. asked his readers to think of him when they were crossing Haystacks, his favourite place

CHAPTER 6

KENDAL MINT CAKE

MORE THAN sixty years ago, a 10-year-old schoolboy called Shane Barron climbed into the bottom of a tea chest with some tins of Kendal Mint Cake, which he proceeded to arrange in layers. He knew that the mint cake – supplied by his grandfather's company, George Romney Ltd – was destined to be taken on an expedition to the Himalayas and Everest. But at that time, Shane couldn't have realised the significance of the trip or the part he was playing in world history. When Edmund Hillary and Tenzing Norgay reached the roof of the world on 29 May 1953, conquering the mountain, they were carrying some of the bars from the supply which Shane had helped to pack. Hillary later recorded that on the summit, he and Norgay embraced each other and then nibbled Kendal Mint Cake. The future fame of the humble mint-flavoured treat was assured. Today, Kendal Mint Cake remains popular with climbers, hikers and adventurers who take it all over the world, as well as visitors to the Lake District who are seeking an injection of sugar and an energy boost in a delicious and portable form. Mint cake wasn't developed as an aid for sportsmen but even today it's still regarded as a type of sports supplement. Of course, lots of people love mint cake for its sugary taste and eat it as they would enjoy any other type of sweet.

Kendal Mint Cake is a curious item of confectionery. It's not actually a cake at all but a mint-flavoured sweet which is usually made in bars and has the consistency of a firm and grainy fudge. It's usually white but can be brown, depending on which type of sugar is used and it can also be made with different flavours. According to popular history, it was discovered by accident when Joseph Wiper, who was making glacier mints, left his cooking pan for too long and noticed that the mixture had begun to turn cloudy instead of clear. He had unwittingly invented Kendal Mint Cake, which he began to manufacture in 1869. Today there are three manufacturers – Romney's, Quiggin's and Wilson's, now part of Creative Confectionery. The firm Wiper's and its mint cake recipes were sold to Romney's in the 1980s and Romney's continues to make Wiper's mint cake alongside its own version.

Shane Barron has now handed the reins at Romney's to his son, John. Both Shane and John have experienced the mint cake effect when they've been on holiday at home or abroad and mentioned what they do: the name Kendal Mint Cake prompts instant recognition and fond smiles as people remember holidays or childhood camping expeditions fuelled by the sweet. John says he's still amazed by how many people know about mint cake and its Everest connections. Shane has distinct memories of growing up and being immersed in the family business. His grandfather, Sam T. Clarke, started Romney's in 1918 and was at the helm when Shane was a schoolboy in Kendal. Shane says Sam was a wonderful man and well regarded for his service as a magistrate, a war-time Special Constable and with The Royal British Legion. Shane had a habit of calling into the factory on his way home from school and on Saturdays. He liked to see his grandfather and an added incentive was that there were always plenty of sweets lying around. Speaking at his home in the Lake District today, he recalls how the British Everest expedition team got in touch with Romney's in 1953 to ask if the firm could supply some mint cake within seven days: 'And grandfather said he would give them so many tea chests.'

As a 10-year-old schoolboy, Shane Barron – pictured at Kendal Castle – helped to pack Kendal Mint Cake carried to the summit of Everest by Edmund Hillary and Tenzing Norgay

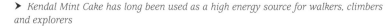
▲ *Kendal Mint Cake is said to have been invented when Joseph Wiper, who was making glacier mints, left the mixture for too long and noticed it had turned cloudy*

➤ *Kendal Mint Cake has long been used as a high energy source for walkers, climbers and explorers*

Rationing was still in force, so the staff gave up their sweet ration coupons to ensure the shipment was legal (the coupons were later refunded by the Ministry of Food) and a shipment of 300 tablets of mint cake was prepared. The mint cake was first put into airtight tins and then came the point at which young Shane climbed inside the tea chests to fulfil his role in preparing the historic shipment: 'I could get inside these tea chests and push them [the tins] in the bottom so they were tight in.' Shane, who was the only one small enough to get inside the chests, packed the first two layers of tins and then the rest of the supplies were added on top. 'When I think back, a hell of a lot of mint cake went into them,' he says. 'They were sealed up in these tea chests and shipped out to base camp in the Himalayas.' At that time, Kendal Mint Cake already had a track record as an ideal foodstuff for expeditions. The key to the sweet's suitability was – and still is – its stability because it doesn't melt in the heat and isn't affected by low temperatures. Shane says: 'If it was cold it didn't freeze. Chocolate is terrible to eat when it's ice cold and terrible to eat when it's hot. That's why the expeditions use it [mint cake] and always have done.' A newspaper advertisement later placed by Romney's explained that the mint cake for the successful Everest attempt had been requested by expedition member George Band, who said it was 'an excellent high-altitude food'.

Shane remembers watching Queen Elizabeth II's coronation on 2 June, on a small television that they had just acquired second-hand, when the news about Hillary and Norgay's achievement came through – although he thinks that his family was told before it was announced to the world at large. The Everest assault meant that mint cake was increasingly in demand for all sorts of trips and expeditions and eventually Romney's had to tell adventurers that they could have supplies at cost but they would have to pay the carriage themselves. The publicity boosted sales but Shane says that it wasn't always good for business because some people wrongly thought that Kendal Mint Cake was a high-energy product, only suitable to be taken on expeditions. 'I suppose if it was launched now that's what you would launch it as, because everybody's interested in high energy,' he says. Although he doesn't run the business nowadays – helping out when he's needed – Shane still eats plenty of mint cake and likes to keep some in the car: 'If you've got a bit drowsy it's the perfect thing to eat as a pick me up; a quick burst of energy.'

Such has been mint cake's association with expeditions and climbing that it was the subject of an exhibition at the town's Museum of Lakeland Life and Industry called Kendal Mint Cake: On Top of the World. The curators interwove the stories of mountaineers and adventurers with the history of mint cake and how it was used to fuel high-level trips. Museum-goers learned how Wiper's mint cake was taken on both the 1922 and 1924 British expeditions to Everest, packed in wooden cases lined with tin. The cases were transported 644km or 400 miles from Darjeeling to base camp by mule. During the expedition, Dr Howard Somervell, who was from Kendal, presented some mint cake to the Dalai Lama, who was responsible for giving permission for expeditions and who was apparently delighted with the gift. George Mallory and Andrew Irvine, who were to sadly perish on the mountain in 1924, were said to be fond of mint cake and the exhibition recorded how Mallory, given the opportunity, would have eaten all the supplies himself. Prior to the Everest assaults, Kendal Mint Cake had been taken on the 1914–17 Imperial Trans-Antarctic Expedition led by Sir Ernest Shackleton. The list of mint cake adventures goes on and mint cake was packed on the RSS *Discovery* for the 1929–31 British, Australian and New Zealand Antarctic Research Expedition. In 1975, the renowned mountaineer Chris Bonington took Quiggin's Kendal Mint Cake on the successful British expedition to Everest. He later wrote that everyone enjoyed the sweet treat when finding something palatable to eat in the extreme cold was difficult. He said that they could also confirm that the mint cake retained its flavour and texture at temperatures of -30°C and below, proving its performance in cold weather. The exhibition in Kendal recorded how, also during 1975, mint cake headed in the other direction when it was taken down a pothole in Papua New Guinea. Its expedition credentials well established, less well known notable moments in mint cake's history include the day in 1970 when Led Zeppelin's Robert Plant and Jimmy Page, who were out for a walk, celebrated writing the song 'That's The Way' by sharing some squares of mint cake. More recently, the actors Ewan McGregor and Charley Boorman packed mint cake for their Long Way Round expedition.

John Barron, Shane Barron's son, is the fourth generation of his family to run Romney's, which employs sixteen people and is still based in Kendal. The firm makes fudge and other confectionery, but mint cake represents 80 per cent of the business. John hasn't done a recent calculation of how many bars the firm produces annually but during 2013 he ordered and used 130 tonnes of sugar. Although mint cake can be produced in white or brown bars, the white remains by far the most popular. Romney's also makes a Winter Candy flavour which tastes of aniseed; Rum and Butter; and Extra Strong Kendal Mint Cake. Some people prefer their mint cake coated in chocolate and Romney's has also started to make chilli mint cake. More recent uses for mint cake include tiny bars served with after-dinner coffee in hotels and restaurants and heart-shaped wedding favours. Walkers love to take mint cake when they're out and about and it was an email from one such customer which prompted some new packaging. The customer said that he liked to have mint cake on his walks but hated it when an opened packet made a mess in his pocket. The answer was a handy tin containing two bars of white or brown mint cake, designed to fit in a walking jacket,

which has been a big success. John claims that mint cake will last for years and years, although the mint flavour will eventually evaporate. Kendal Mint Cake doesn't have a long or complicated list of ingredients and despite its lengthy shelf life it doesn't contain preservatives. In fact, the ingredients for white and brown mint cake alike are simply sugar, glucose syrup, water and peppermint oil. The peppermint oil is what gives the mint cake its distinctive taste – and if you visit a mint cake factory it will also make your eyes water and clear your sinuses. The secret to producing Kendal Mint Cake is in how it's made. John says it's all to do with the temperature at which the sugar, water and glucose syrup are boiled in a mixing vessel (the peppermint oil is added later) and then, crucially, the method with which it's stirred or agitated – which is called graining. 'In the graining process, you'll see it turning from a clear to a slightly cloudy consistency,' says John. 'If you don't do it enough, it comes out sticky and if you do too much, it comes out very crumbly.' After years spent in the business, John and his colleagues are skilled at graining, knowing exactly when the mint cake mixture is ready. The copper pans used for this part of the process are about sixty years old and perform better than any other type. After graining, a pan filled with mint cake mixture is placed on a trolley and then wheeled down a series of long tables, on which silicone moulds have been lined up. As he pushes the trolley along the tables, John uses a ladle to dish out the mixture and pours out exactly the right amount each time, quickly filling the moulds before the mint cake can begin to set. After about ten minutes the mint cake is ready and the moulds can be turned out. All that then remains to do is to package the sweet.

John grew up working in the business but as a young man he went off to try other things before coming back to mint cake production. By then he says he had begun to appreciate the history and heritage of his family's association with the sweet. He hopes that mint cake production can continue in Kendal, unlike other traditional manufacturing which the

An original Wilson's mint cake recipe, an old-style bar and a replica ice axe of the type used by George Mallory in the 1920s, courtesy of Mountain Heritage Trust, on display at the Museum of Lakeland Life and Industry in Kendal

town has lost: 'You can see there's a tradition there you don't want to lose. I would love to see it carrying on, especially with all the businesses that have gone in Kendal. Now I do feel a lot for it.' John and his family enjoy getting out and about and mint cake goes with them: 'I do a lot of walking and it's an ideal thing to put in your backpack.' Demand for Romney's mint cake has been increasing recently and it's stocked by some major outdoor stores. An agent who supplies outdoor companies with the latest energy bars approached Romney's to secure mint cake for the same market. 'You've got all your energy gels and for us to keep going alongside them is pretty impressive,' says John. Perhaps despite all the innovations in sports technology, the sweet that powered Hillary and Tenzing to the top of the world is still thought to be good enough for most of our everyday outdoor adventures.

▲ *Mint cake takes about ten minutes to set*

▶ *John Barron is the fourth generation of his family to make the famous sugary sweet*

Shane Barron says he often thinks about the part Romney's mint cake played in world history and the time when he helped to pack the sweet in tea chests to be transported to Everest base camp. The story has passed into history and tends to crop up from time to time on television, or perhaps as a quiz question. Shane says brown is his favourite mint cake and he enjoys finding some stowed in his golf bag. The Everest expedition is featured on the reverse of Romney's wrappers and customers still like to talk about the mint cake's role on the roof of the world. As Shane says: 'It's been part of our life.'

CHAPTER 7

LAKELAND'S FOOTPATHS

HEADS DOWN and braced against howling winds and horizontal rain, four bedraggled men carrying a coffin made their way up a steep, zigzagged path. Their climb took them away from their homes in Mardale Green village in the valley below them. Ahead of them was an 11km or 7-mile trek across Swindale, leading eventually to the village of Shap. Stopping at a particular point, they eased the coffin on to a flat-topped stone – still there today and known as Resting Howe – while they rubbed their aching arms and caught their breaths. Not stopping for long, they took up their burden once more and marched onwards to their destination. This scene could have happened at any point during the village's history until the early eighteenth century, when the church at Mardale was granted its own burial rights. Until then, the nearest cemetery had been at the larger church in Shap. Each time there was a death in Mardale, the tortuous journey would have been undertaken, whatever the weather, as the men of the village carried their dead family and friends to where they could receive a Christian burial. The last recorded use of the route was on 7 June 1736, when John Holme was taken along the path to his final resting place.

The path, which is now a bridleway along its whole length, is well used today by some of the millions of recreational walkers who take to the Lake District's fells each year. It's known as the Old Corpse Road, despite it subsequently being used for different purposes. As Paul Hindle points out in *Roads and Tracks of the Lake District*, by 1860, when the railway had reached Shap, Mardale was sending 1,360kg or 3,000lb of butter to Manchester each week. The butter may well have taken the same route

as the corpses from previous centuries. Presumably the Old Butter Road didn't have the same ring as the more dramatic sounding name. The great walking author Alfred Wainwright had an alternative explanation for the route's existence. He speculated that the steep zigzagged path, which was constructed that way to help ease the gradient, was probably created as a route for bringing down peat – then the main source of fuel – from Mardale Common. Whatever the truth, the Old Corpse Road is the name that's persisted.

The village of Mardale Green became well known in its own right when, in the mid-1930s, the seventy occupants had to abandon their homes. The village was 'drowned' to allow the level of Haweswater to be raised to create a reservoir which would supply water for people in Manchester. The church was dismantled and 100 corpses, buried there since the early eighteenth century, were dug up and reinterred at Shap. Wainwright enjoyed the irony of what happened: '… thus reuniting the remains of the more recent dead with those of their ancestors who came the hard way along the Old Corpse Road.'

The Old Corpse Road is one small but well-known section of a vast network of paths, bridleways and other routes which snake across the Lake District and Cumbria. It's also an illustration of what Nick Thorne, countryside access adviser for the Lake District National Park Authority, says about such routes. 'Footpaths don't exist by accident; they're there for a reason. Most of them went somewhere.' The Lake District National Park's rights of way extend to 3,100km or 1,926 miles. There are 2,167km or 1,346 miles of public footpaths, 888km (552 miles) of

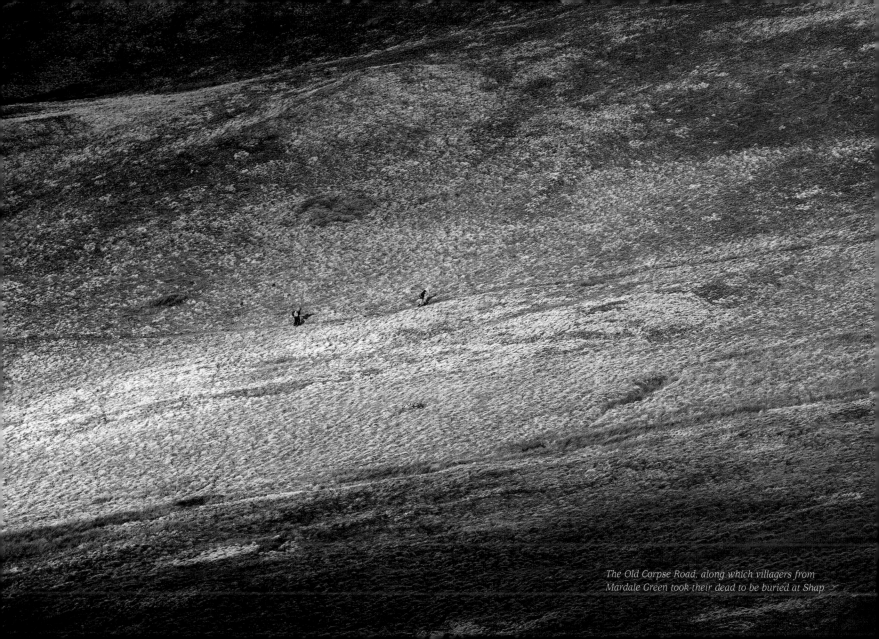

The Old Corpse Road, along which villagers from
Mardale Green took their dead to be buried at Shap

Resting Howe, the large stone on the zigzagged path above Mardale, is thought to have been the spot where a coffin could be rested while its carriers caught their breaths

▲ *A wooden post marks the route for walkers on the Old Corpse Road*

➤ *Today the Old Corpse Road is popular with walkers*

public bridleways, 30km (19 miles) of byways open to all traffic and 15km (9 miles) of restricted byways – which are the same as byways but can't be used by cars and motorbikes. Cumbria as a whole has 7,630km or 4,741 miles of rights of way. There are 3,500 finger posts in the national park and many thousands of the small arrows attached to posts which point the way for walkers. In an average year, the Lake District National Park Authority processes twelve legal changes to the mapped routes; carries out 500 practical tasks on rights of way to maintain or improve them; improves up to 150 stiles, gates and other features of paths to make them easier to use and surveys a quarter of the rights of way network. Nick says that many of the historic battles over rights of way and access took place in the north-west. The large expanses of countryside located

Stockley Bridge, a landmark on Sty Head Pass

next to cities where working people toiled in poor conditions may have had something to do with this.

The Lake District is also one of the places where the concept of walking for pleasure developed. The Romantic poets, William Wordsworth and Samuel Taylor Coleridge, were known for composing poetry while they walked. The letters of Wordsworth's sister, Dorothy, who was an important third person in the friendship, are studded with references to walking. Walking from one place to a destination must have often been a necessity but it's clear that, just as it is for ramblers today, a walk of several hours was regarded with pleasure by the Wordsworths. In a letter to William's future wife, Mary Hutchinson, in 1801, Dorothy writes: 'We had such a walk! So delightful! We left Keswick at ½ past 5 in order that we might avoid the heat of the day, and we rested again and again by the road-side. We had the full round moon before us just above Helvellyn.' Dorothy and William had been visiting Coleridge and arrived home at Grasmere at midnight, six-and-a-half hours after setting out.

In a letter to a friend in September 1800, not long after the siblings had settled in Grasmere, she explains that they walk every day, 'and at all times of the day'. She continues: 'We are daily more delighted with Grasmere, and its neighbourhood; our walks are perpetually varied, and we are more fond of the mountains as our acquaintance with them increases.' Nick Thorne says the idea that walking could be undertaken as a pleasurable activity in its own right really took off thanks to the Romantic poets: 'Wordsworth walked thousands of miles in the Lake District. He obviously got inspiration from being out for a walk and then wrote and this encouraged others to go out and about and get the same experiences.'

For Nick, the development of our footpaths makes them a vital part of the history of modern life: 'That's why I think the rights of way network is so important. It's as much our cultural heritage as stately homes, farms, factories, industries and canals. You can walk the routes people have been walking for a long time and possibly many thousands of years.' The adoption of walking for pleasure was soon followed by arguments about access. A mass 'invasion' of Kinder Scout in Derbyshire took place in 1932, with hundreds of people demanding access rights to the land. More than forty years before that, walkers had taken the same action on land around Keswick. The countryside champion Canon Hardwicke Drummond Rawnsley, who went on to become one of the founders of the National Trust, had revived an organisation which he called the Keswick and District Footpath Preservation Society. In one of its early documents, he wrote that the association had become necessary because of the 'imperative need' of preserving the 'national inheritance' of ancient rights of way, roadside strips and village greens. 'There is each year an increasing desire on the part of all classes of the public to make use of these quiet bye-ways for healthful recreation, for art studies, for natural history research, for thought, and for exercise,' he wrote. Rawnsley pointed out that many paths were being closed against the wishes and the best interests of a whole neighbourhood: 'It would be needless to point out how, in this neighbourhood especially, the public rights of way as well as the private rights of owners of property need safe-guarding.'

*Sty Head Pass, on the flanks of Great Gable, links
the Lakeland valleys of Wasdale and Borrowdale*

The society organised a mass protest in October 1887, when 2,000 people took to the fells in a stand against the closure of all the routes up Latrigg above the town. The protest led to court action and eventually a compromise, which secured the Spooney Green access to Latrigg. However, despite these early protests, it wasn't until the 1949 National Parks and Access to the Countryside Act that a comprehensive record of all the rights of way in the country was put together. Although the process was far from perfect and a number of rights of way weren't recorded and were therefore lost, without the Act many more footpaths could have been closed to the public over the last fifty years.

Access restrictions weren't the only threat to some of the Lake District's footpaths. The Lake District is home to a number of high mountain passes or routes which enable walkers – and sometimes cars – to cross high ranges and so move from one valley to the next. A famous pass is Sty Head, which is popular with walkers travelling between Borrowdale and Wasdale Head. Sty Head, which means 'the top of the ladder', is a relatively short walk of about 7km or 4 miles, but motorists face a circuitous journey of many times that distance. It was partly this which led to the now almost unbelievable proposal to build a road over the pass. Such a route would have cut the driving distance from Keswick to Wastwater from 90km, or 56 miles, to 27km, or 17 miles. The scheme would have involved replacing the track with a metalled road which could be used by carriages, cyclists and motorcars. The idea was first discussed in the 1890s and a road over Sty Head continued to be a live issue well into the twentieth century.

John Musgrove, of Whitehaven, who was a lawyer and industrialist, was behind the initial idea. He bought land on either side of the pass and pressed the county council – where the county surveyor, George Bell was supportive – to help pay for the £10,000 scheme. People who were already involved in defending Lakeland came out against the plan. In their book The Lake Counties, John Duncan Marshall and John K. Walton explain that the plan wouldn't have suited the area's tourism businesses any more than it would the conservationists:

Canon Rawnsley was particularly assiduous in his attacks on the road plan, pointing out that any public money invested would merely provide undue private benefits for Musgrave and that the scheme, which involved new hotels at Sty Head and Seascale, would bring competition for the existing accommodation industry without any compensating benefits.

Those who supported the road included cyclists and motorists and people who believed that everyone was entitled to enjoy the Lake District. The West Cumberland Times pointed out that at the end of the nineteenth century, only 1 per cent of visitors saw the magnificent views from Sty Head. The newspaper said that those who were able to enjoy the view should be prepared to share it with others. The plan failed through, according to Marshall and Walton, 'a combination of inertia and vested interests'. Although today there are roads over other passes, Sty Head remains inaccessible to motorists. On fine days it's thronged with walkers and is busier than Wainwright – who must bear a lot of the responsibility for the route's popularity – would ideally have liked. He wrote of the pass: 'Sty Head is a sanctuary of silence and peace amongst the grandest mountains in the country and should remain so.'

In the same piece of writing about Sty Head, Wainwright alluded to a problem which was first identified in the early nineteenth century, was causing real difficulties by the 1960s and which has continued to be an issue for the Lake District. He wrote: 'This is a part of Lakeland that has never changed. Today's visitors see it as it has always been; to an old man it appears just as it was in the days of his youth, only the paths can show evidence of greater use and the cairns have grown in size.' Footpath erosion and damage to the mountain environment, caused by the boots of some of the millions of visitors to the Lake District each year, is ugly and can lead to loss of habitat, water pollution and damage to an area's archaeology. Fix the Fells, an organisation set up to help address the issues, has traced the problem's history. In 1819, a traveller arriving at The Old Dungeon Ghyll in the Langdale Valley complained that the route was in a much worse state than on his last visit. The routes were then part of the local economy and were repaired by those who used them, including packmen, miners and landowners. During the 1940s, visitors increasingly used cars to access the Lake District but by the 1960s, more people were taking to the fells for leisure walking and scars began to appear on the most popular routes. Years of experimenting with repairs followed until a set of guidelines was established by the Access Management Group (AMG) – made up by the Lake District National Park Authority, the National Trust and what's now called Natural England.

The AMG secured lottery funding to repair 102 paths and set up Fix the Fells using a second lottery grant. About 100 volunteers now turn out regularly to help with the work. Different techniques have included soil inversion, which involves turning over the top few feet of soil so that the stone underneath provides a firmer surface. A raised path with a ditch either side for drainage is then created. Stone pitching, or surfacing paths with stone, is another option when helicopters are used to bring in the stones. One of the first pitched paths to be constructed was at Sty Head. Work is also continuing to improve features on the paths. Stiles – unless they are of some particular merit because of their age or construction or historical significance – are often replaced by gates to help ensure less mobile people can access the fells. As the national park authority, Nick Thorne and his colleagues work to balance the rights of landowners and walkers, enabling access and trying to ensure as little conflict as possible.

When foot-and-mouth disease took hold in the countryside in early 2001, it led to the wholesale closure of footpaths in Cumbria. There was an immediate, devastating and ultimately long-lasting impact on the county's tourism industry. Nick says the closure had an unexpected benefit as it changed some people's perceptions of footpaths. It was realised how vital they were to the county's economy and way of life. Since that time, it has been easier to find co-operation and funding for work to improve the network. Nick says that footpaths, which are among the oldest features in the landscape, help to connect us to our roots. When you stride out on the Old Corpse Road from Mardale or take to Sty Head Pass, you're only the latest in a long line of walkers before you. 'You get a feeling you're doing something hundreds and hundreds of your ancestors have also done.'

The pitched stone path meanders its way to Sty Head Pass

CHAPTER 8

BEATRIX POTTER

I F BEATRIX POTTER'S family had decided to visit Scotland in 1882 instead of Windermere, her life and the history of the Lake District would have been very different. The wealthy London family usually decamped north of the border for the summer but when the rent for their holiday home was increased, Beatrix's father instead booked Wray Castle on the western shore of Windermere. Beatrix, who was 16, encountered the flora and fauna, villages, lakes and fells which were to feature in so many of the 'little books' for which she became famous and which made her fortune. That summer at Wray was also significant because she met Hardwicke Drummond Rawnsley, a young and enthusiastic clergyman who inspired Beatrix with his passion for the landscape. He went on to become one of the founders of the National Trust and Beatrix was to become one of the foremost protectors of the Lake District. Between them, the two friends did much to shape the Lake District that exists today.

When she died in 1943 Beatrix left behind an enduring literary legacy which included twenty-three 'little books', as they became known, such as *The Tale of Peter Rabbit* and also *Mrs Tiggy-Winkle*, *Squirrel Nutkin* and *Benjamin Bunny*. She also left a second legacy for the nation, bequeathing 4,300 acres of land and sixty individual properties, including fifteen farms, to the National Trust. The gift helped to protect the landscape and also highlighted its unique ecological importance. It's never been forgotten and in 2005, sixty years after her death, the National Trust was criticised for splitting up High Yewdale Farm at Coniston, where the tenant farmer had retired. Opponents said it should have been kept intact as Beatrix had left it, although at the time the Trust argued that the author would have understood the need for change.

The author's most recent biographer, the environmental historian Dr Linda Lear, believes that Beatrix's impact on the landscape of the Lake District was matched by the effect that same landscape had on her books. The stories and illustrations draw heavily on Lake District scenery, the hamlet of Near Sawrey where she eventually settled and her garden at Hill Top, her first home in the area. In fact nine of the books published between 1905 and 1913 are set in and around Hill Top. The garden appears in *The Tale of Tom Kitten* and *Jemima Puddle-Duck* and the village features in *Puddle-Duck* and *The Tale of Ginger and Pickles*. Nearby Esthwaite Water and Moss Eccles Tarn can be seen in *The Tale of Mr Jeremy Fisher*. Further afield, Newlands Valley near Keswick appears in *Mrs Tiggy-Winkle*. Speaking from her home in the USA, Linda says: 'Her books are admired not only for her clever plots and characters but because of their beautifully rendered settings which include the plants and animals that she knew first-hand. Those settings are unique to the Lake District.'

The tale of how Beatrix Potter found fame against all the odds and her own inclinations is as captivating and original as one of her stories. She had originally resorted to self-publishing her first children's book, but they went on to sell millions of copies and to be translated into more

➤ *Tower Bank Arms in the village of Near Sawrey is hardly changed from when it appeared in Beatrix Potter's* The Tale of Jemima Puddle-Duck

Esthwaite Water inspired a setting in The Tale of Mr Jeremy Fisher

than thirty languages. The books remain popular today and Hill Top, near Hawkshead, is a tourist attraction. A replica of the house has even been built at a children's zoo in Tokyo, nearly 6,000 miles away.

Beatrix was a woman of contradictions. Brought up in a city, she had a lifelong fascination with animals and plants. She was an offcomer but was one of the most significant figures in the Lake District's development. She created charming stories about the adventures of animals which usually had happy endings and yet when her childhood pets died, their bodies were boiled so that she could study and make accurate drawings of their anatomies. She was also the product of a Victorian upbringing but had an easy grasp of scientific ideas and loved the study of natural history. One particular paradox which has fascinated her readers is that although Beatrix was able to communicate with youngsters through her books, she married too late to have children of her own and isn't remembered by some who knew her when they were children as being particularly friendly to young people.

Beatrix was raised in Kensington in London. She and her brother, Bertram, were permitted to keep a menagerie of animals at home which included rabbits, guinea pigs and less conventionally a lizard, hedgehog, mice and bats. She made drawings of these pets and was eventually able to produce accurate anatomical sketches. Linda Lear, who wrote *Beatrix Potter: The Extraordinary Life of a Victorian Genius*, says that when the family left London to holiday in the countryside, Beatrix experienced a freedom she wasn't usually allowed at home, where she was always accompanied by a governess or parent. 'At Dalguise in Scotland or in the Lake District she's allowed to take her pony and trap by herself and explore the countryside. I think the freedom to discover and explore was vital to her intellectual outlook as well as her artistic eye. For someone as curious as Potter, it was essential.' It's possible that her appreciation of Scotland and the Lake District was also connected to her family's northern roots, as both her parents' families were from Lancashire and had made money in the Manchester cotton trade. Beatrix was aware and proud of her origins and was later to write that although she was born in London, her family's joy and interests were in the north country.

Her upbringing was regimented and adhered to many of the Victorian conventions of the time. She was encouraged in her love of drawing and painting and she continued to record the world around her and the plants and animals she encountered both in her journal and in her art. As she grew older, her skill in botanical drawings and her interest in fungi developed to such an extent that she visited experts at the Natural History Museum and the Royal Botanic Gardens at Kew. She wrote a paper on the germination of spores and in 1897 it was presented to The Linnean Society – an august natural history society which still exists today. Women were not allowed to be members or to take part in meetings, so Beatrix wasn't there in person when her paper was put forward. Linda says she was interested in all the natural sciences and dared to advance her own ideas in botany against the social conventions of that time. 'She was ahead of her time in much of the natural sciences. If women had been allowed to join The Linnean Society and she had given her paper herself – and if she had been able to do further research and correct it,

Little Town, nestling in Newlands Valley, provided a setting for The Tale of Mrs Tiggy-Winkle

Castle Cottage in Near Sawrey, where Beatrix set up home with William Heelis following their marriage

if she had got any support from any of the male scientists at the Natural History Museum or Kew – I have no doubt she would have gone on to be a successful botanist. That was not to be.' Instead, Beatrix focused her observational and artistic skills creatively, writing and illustrating her books and forging a career. After she moved to the Lake District, her interest in animals and science didn't abate. She became a farmer and a champion breeder of Herdwick sheep, the Lake District's native breed. Invited to judge the breed at agricultural shows, she was one of the first female members of the Herdwick Sheep Breeders' Association and was named president-elect in 1943, although she died before she could take on the role. Linda says she was again ahead of her time in treating her sheep, advocating for the latest veterinarian medicines and

disease prevention techniques for her Herdwicks. Her research in fungi had alerted her to the properties of penicillin before its official discovery. 'Her stories generally have happy endings but in real life she's acquainted with animals that get lost, get hurt, fall off a cliff, or freeze to death in snow,' says Linda.

Hill Top was a working farm and as Beatrix's books became more successful, she was able to make improvements, buy stock and purchase more land. In 1913, when she was 47, she married a local solicitor called William Heelis. Beatrix had already bought Castle Cottage Farm, across the road from Hill Top, and that became their marital home. She later bought the 2,000-acre Troutbeck Park Farm near Windermere, which gave her more standing among the farming community.

Willow Taylor, who was born in 1923 and grew up in Near Sawrey, is one of the last people to remember Beatrix. Willow's parents ran the Tower Bank Arms in the hamlet. Without any traffic to worry about, Willow and her friends played ball games on the main road through the village. When the ball was knocked over the wall into Post Office Meadow, which was owned by Beatrix, Willow would climb over to claim it back.

Willow recalls how Beatrix would then arrive and admonish her for not using the gate. The little girl wouldn't answer back but might mutter under her breath. The usual outcome was that Beatrix would go to Willow's father and tell him how naughty his daughter had been, so that she was kept inside for the rest of the day. Even today Willow says of the author: 'Crabby old thing, we used to think. She didn't stop or chat to us, she wasn't all that fond of children. Although she wrote those beautiful books for children, she wasn't fond of them – they were a bit of a nuisance.' Linda Lear defends Beatrix – who by that time would have been in her 60s – and says that her correspondence and real-life relationships with several youngsters shows that she did in fact like children. She adored her husband's nieces and nephews, for example, wrote stories for them and helped with their education. She would have expected children to be well-behaved and well-mannered however, and so wouldn't have appreciated youngsters climbing over dry stone walls, which took many hours to construct.

Beatrix fell in love with Sawrey in 1896 when she was 30 and the Potter family rented a house for the summer called Lakefield, just outside the village above Esthwaite Water. When she was able to buy her own property in the Lake District, it was this area that she chose. 'She thought Esthwaite Water was the most beautiful of the lakes,' says Linda. 'I don't think she looked anywhere else; she only looked at that little village. She had had the word out for quite some time that she wanted to buy property there.' There was also a family connection, because her great-grandfather had once owned property nearby in Coniston and such associations were important to her. Eventually, when she bought the 4,000-acre Monk Coniston estate, the farm was to belong to her. Like many people who have settled in the Lakes, she also found peace and quiet in her surroundings. 'She was a very shy, retiring person all her life who enjoyed solitary pursuits,' says Linda. 'When you think of what Beatrix Potter did with her time, she paints, she reads, she writes, she gardens, she walks in the countryside, she observes. She's not outgoing; she has few friends, either as an adult or child.' One long-standing friend was Hardwicke Rawnsley and Linda says their relationship was interwoven with her feelings about the Lake District:

The countryside stole her heart straight away. I think initially it had a lot to do with Rawnsley and meeting him and with sharing his inherent love of the Lake District. He was fighting the railways and starting to fight for Lake District preservation and she shared his vision from the start.

◄ *Willow Taylor, who grew up in Near Sawrey, is one of the last people to have known Beatrix Potter*

▼ *The scenery in and around her home in Near Sawrey, such as this beech wood, provided inspiration for Beatrix Potter's famous children's stories*

Having won admiration for her children's books, in later life she became recognised locally as a successful farmer and prize-winning sheep breeder. It's hard to think of another woman of her generation who achieved excellence in such diverse areas as children's literature, natural science and agriculture. Her legacy to the National Trust remains one of the largest and most important and included a clause that the landlord's flocks on her farms were to remain pure Herdwick. A farmer at her funeral was heard to remark that it was a 'bad day' for farmers. A town-bred offcomer, she had done more than enough to earn the respect of her neighbours.

When she died, in December 1943, the notice in the local newspaper said nothing of her careers as an author or farmer, recording only that she was the dearly loved wife of William Heelis and only daughter of the late Rupert Potter. The cremation was to be private, the notice said, and there was a request for no flowers, no letters and no mourning. To the end, Beatrix hoped to maintain her privacy. Willie, who was left broken-hearted, died in 1945.

Today Lake District tourists, fans and holidaymakers can visit Hill Top and view Beatrix's original artwork at the Beatrix Potter Gallery, which is housed in William Heelis' former law office in Hawkshead. They can take their children to The World of Beatrix Potter Attraction in Bowness-on-Windermere and see recreations of scenes from her books. At the Armitt Museum in Ambleside there are many examples of her drawings and watercolours of fungi and scholars come from all over the world to look at her work. Visitors to the Lake District also have ample choice of souvenirs to take home.

It's impossible to know for sure what would have happened if, in 1882, the Potter family had been able to rent their usual Scottish holiday home and hadn't taken Wray Castle. However, not only would Beatrix not have discovered the Lake District landscape but she wouldn't have met Hardwicke Rawnsley. The irony is that the Lake District, where she found peace and solitude, helped to provide the literary inspiration which made her famous and which in turn paid for her to purchase land and farms which she left to the nation through the National Trust.

Beatrix Potter fulfilled a long-held wish when she moved to the village of Near Sawrey

Everything about her dual legacies resulted from her falling in love with Sawrey, with Esthwaite Water and with the Lakes. Linda Lear says: 'You have a sense in her life of her yearning to find this place and the freedom that it gave. It's the countryside she's in love with and it's this particular countryside that she adores like no other.'

CHAPTER 9

THE CLIMBERS

Chris Bonington, Dave Birkett and Leo Houlding

THEY'VE REACHED the roof of the world, climbed in the most inhospitable terrains and climates that the earth has to offer and seen sights so stunning that most of us couldn't conjure them from our imaginations. But home for Sir Chris Bonington and Leo Houlding is a corner of north-west England, where the mightiest mountain, Scafell Pike, at 978m or 3,210ft, is a molehill compared to the peaks that they've conquered.

Their fellow climber, Dave Birkett, has achieved unparalleled success on the crags of his native Lake District, an area to which he is as attached as the indigenous Herdwick sheep that he plucks from danger when they become crag fast.

Born in 1934, Chris Bonington is now seen as the elder statesman of mountaineering and exploration. He made the first British ascent of the north face of the Eiger and in 1975 led the first ascent of the south-west face of Everest before reaching the world's highest peak himself a decade later, when he was 50. From the 1960s to the '90s, he chalked up first ascents in the Himalayas, the Alps, Patagonia, Pakistan, China, Greenland and Tibet, leading nineteen expeditions to the Himalayas alone. When he compares the Lake District with other places, he knows what he's talking about: 'I love the Lakes. It's as beautiful as anywhere in the world; it's as wonderful as anywhere in the world. There are many, many places that are incredibly beautiful, whether it's the mountains of the Alps, whether it's the Nepalese Himalayas, whether it's down in Patagonia. The Lakes stand out.' The Lake District has everything Chris wants but in a compact area: 'The extraordinary thing about the Lake District is it can be so beautiful and yet so very, very small.'

Chris' friend, Leo Houlding, represents the current generation of climbers. Born in 1980, he grew up near Appleby in Cumbria. Often described as a climbing prodigy, he was just 10 when he made headlines by becoming the youngest person to climb the Old Man of Hoy sea stack off Orkney – coincidentally first climbed in 1966 by Chris Bonington. Leo's breathtaking exploits in Yosemite in California made his name in the climbing world and he's become known for BASE jumping from fixed points and para-alpinism – that is, climbing a mountain and then flying down. Like Chris, he has stood on the roof of the world after conquering Everest as part of an expedition to make a film, *The Wildest Dream*, which recreated Irvine and Mallory's ill-fated 1924 attempt on the summit. Leo even wore 1920s-style tweed clothing for part of the climb. In 2013 he led a team to the north-east ridge of Ulvetanna – Norwegian for 'the wolf's tooth' – in eastern Antarctica, regarded as the most technically demanding peak on the harshest continent. As his exploits have become more daring, his media profile has increased and he's appeared on television's *Top Gear* and presented a children's science programme called *Fierce Earth*. He's already a veteran of the lecture circuit and in 2013 his career took him to thirty countries, while he still made time to climb on seven continents.

During his Cumbrian childhood, Leo learned to climb with his father. He's also lived in the climbing heartlands of North Wales and the Peak District but he and his doctor wife, Jessica, have chosen to come home to the Lake District. Leo says:

Sir Chris Bonington, the elder statesman of British mountaineering and an international figure in his sport

There's so much to do right on the doorstep. I've had the privilege of going to many of the most beautiful corners of the earth, amazing natural wonders and I mean it sincerely that when I get back from Antarctica or the Amazon or Yosemite and I drive back here, on the right day, it's magnificent; it's as wonderful as anywhere in the world.'

The Lake District is named for its lakes but its high fells and peaks are what have attracted many over the years. It's also long been regarded as the spiritual home of rock climbing, which is often said to have become a sport in its own right in June 1886, when Walter Parry Haskett Smith made his solo ascent of Napes Needle, the jutting and forbidding pinnacle on Great Gable. Although home to England's highest peak – Scafell Pike – the Lake District doesn't have dizzying heights compared to other places at home or abroad. Scafell Pike itself is shorter than its sister peaks, Snowdon in Wales and Ben Nevis in Scotland. And yet the Lake District continues to be a special place for many climbers.

Chris Bonington – who has been Sir Chris since 1996 when his services to mountaineering were rewarded with a knighthood – first came to the area during the Second World War when his school was evacuated to Kirkby Lonsdale, a market town that today lies on the border of Cumbria and Lancashire. He spent school holidays in Grasmere and can remember taking a boat out on the lake with his grandmother and effectively marooning her on an island when she dozed off and he rowed away, much to her annoyance. More significantly, he remembers going for walks which could now be seen as the first baby steps in what was to be an illustrious career: 'I remember walking up to see Grizedale Tarn and walking a little way up Fairfield. It was a minimal trek up, no more.'

Chris and his wife, Wendy, settled in Cumbria and now live at Hesket Newmarket in the northern fells. For Chris, part of the appeal of the Lake District is that the landscape isn't a wilderness: the hand of man has been an influence for 4,000 years. The Lakeland fells look the way they are because they've been grazed by sheep and because of the dry stone walls which have turned the fells into a patchwork landscape. Those in charge have largely done a good job of preserving the landscape, he believes, particularly by controlling the amount and type of building.

Over the last forty years, Chris has seen footpath erosion increase and salutes the organisations which have tackled the scars that have opened up on the fells. But that hasn't altered his view that the Lake District is for everyone to enjoy.

I think with places like the Lake District and places of natural beauty it's very, very important that ordinary people have access to them. Huge numbers of people come to the Lakes. I think the extraordinary thing is, in spite of those large numbers – and some don't get very far from the road – they gain an enormous amount just from being here.

The challenge is to ensure that people can enjoy the Lakes without damaging the very thing they've come to see, he says.

Local people also need to be able to make a living and have a good life in the Lakes and tourism plays a vital part in that. Chris stepped down from his role as vice president of the conservation charity, Friends of the Lake District, over the group's opposition to a zip wire that the owners of Honister Slate Mine wanted to set up in the Borrowdale Valley. Chris says that since the first climbers came to the area in the late nineteenth century, young people have sought out exciting things to do in the Lake District. Today that might include a zip wire: 'It's exciting, it gives a good adrenalin rush and it's scary but if it's attracting people to the Lakes and it's not doing any damage – which it doesn't – I think there's nothing wrong with it.'

Aside from the landscape, Chris admires Cumbria's strong communities and spirit, which have led like-minded adventurers to join him in the Lake District: 'More and more climbers come and live here; there's no shortage of people to climb with.' He and Wendy plan to stay where they are: 'We would never move from here.'

As a member of the last generation to learn his sport before climbing walls made it more accessible, Leo Houlding says that he was fortunate to grow up in Cumbria. Being able to get on to the fells was a vital part of learning to climb. One of his first climbs was on The Hoff outcrop, close to his home near Appleby. As a teenager he climbed on Reecastle in Borrowdale, which remains a favourite area: 'They were the first hard routes I ever did when I was 15; they're still hard.'

Leo and his wife, Jessica, could live anywhere but he appreciates the subtle beauty of the Lake District, where it's possible to notice the moss on the walls in a way that it's not amid the towering monoliths of Yosemite in California. 'I like the Lake District,' he says. 'What I do appreciate and a lot of people don't realise, is what a privileged quality of life it is here. I travel a lot in the Third World and all over the world – this year I've been to thirty countries and climbed on seven continents – and the quality of life here is as good as anywhere in the world without question. The lack of crime, the education and healthcare, quiet roads. It's really unique.' Like Chris Bonington, he recognises that the area is reliant on tourism: 'The catch is, there's no economy.' To live in the Lake District means having to find a niche.

The Lake District's mountains are tiny by Leo's standards. But he says that for climbers, the challenge often lies in finding the most difficult way up. In the summer of 2013, Leo climbed Deer Bield in Easedale in the Lake District. From a distance, it looks 'completely insignificant', he says, but once a climber gets close it becomes clear that it's as good a test as anything in Yosemite. 'Most people wouldn't even see this buttress but once you get up close and personal, even though it's only 10 metres long, it's 10 metres of magic,' he says. 'That sums up Lake District climbing.'

Leo came home to the Lakes and Chris Bonington chose to make the area his home. But Dave Birkett, one of the most talented rock climbers the UK has ever produced, is as hefted to the Lake District as one of the area's native Herdwick sheep. He's also regarded by many as the ultimate Lake District climber. When he made the first ascent of his route, If Six Was Nine, on Iron Crag above Thirlmere, it was said to be the hardest crag ridge in the world at that time. It took fifteen years before someone repeated it and it hasn't had a third ascent.

Dave grew up in the Langdales and now lives half a mile, as the crow flies, from the house where he was born. He is the third generation of his family to reach the top in rock climbing: his paternal grandfather, Jim Birkett, was one of the finest climbers of his day and dominated the sport from the 1930s to the '50s. His uncle, Bill Birkett, became known for his climbing and for his photography and writing, producing many books on the Lake District and other landscapes. Dave's maternal grandfather, Vic Gregg, was a well-regarded farmer of Herdwick sheep and Vic's father, Joe, was also a Herdwick specialist who advised Beatrix Potter, the children's author-turned-Herdwick farmer. Dave's Lake District credentials are hard to beat. Dave's climbing has taken him across the world but he regards the decade he spent forging routes on Scafell as his greatest sporting achievement. Of the eight first ascents he made on the mountain, only one has ever been repeated.

His day job also revolves around the geology of the Lakes and he makes his living as a stonemason, repairing dry stone walls and crafting specialist stone features. His skill is such that his stone work featured in the best show garden at the Chelsea Flower Show in 2012. He admires the rocky landscape in which he works and plays, praising the quality of rocks on certain crags as phenomenal. His first experiences of being in high places in the Lakes were with his maternal grandfather, farmer Vic Gregg, who would take a young Dave with him to rescue sheep: 'I used to love being on the farm. All the time through school at lambing time and hay time I was taken out of school. The big thing was rescuing sheep off the crags. My grandfather used to lower me down on ropes. That was my first introduction to climbing.' Dave has strived to be on the fells ever since: 'Being in the fells has always been it.' He doesn't try to over-analyse what the fells mean to him but it's clear it includes a sense of perspective: 'The earliest memories are from when you look down. Things seem very small. It's always been that kind of escapism; it doesn't have to be climbing, it can be just walking, clearing your head.'

His first real climb was in the Langdales when he was about 16. He remembers the feelings he encountered when tackling White Ghyll, a sheer rock face that looks terrifying to non-climbers and proved to be so for a young Dave. He recalls saying to himself: 'Why am I here? Just get me out of here God and I won't do it again.' But it wasn't long before the

Leo Houlding learned to climb as a schoolboy in Cumbria and is known for cutting-edge climbs and audacious expeditions. His prowess as a climber and explorer has been captured on film and television

terror was forgotten and he was climbing again: 'All of a sudden you get to the bottom and you know what? You're in exactly the same position, saying "why am I doing this?"' But despite these times, climbing isn't something Dave does for the adrenalin rush but rather for a moment when everything comes together and the feeling is magical.

Dave has climbed in other places and has followed his sport all over the UK and overseas. He was the first person to climb E9 routes – regarded as being at the very limit of what's physically possible for top climbers – in England, Wales, Scotland and Ireland. Only one person has matched that achievement. Yet he's quiet about his climbing record and he can't tell you how many first ascents he's done: 'It's not as many as a lot of people. I've not been interested in doing what I would think are average routes. Some people are new-route mad – I'm not, I want to do quality climbs.' He seems more satisfied about continuing the work he started on his grandfather's farm by finding crag fast sheep and bringing them safely home. Farmers call him when they lose their animals and Dave turns out, often taking time off work. He never accepts money for what he does. He reckons he's saved about 600 sheep, plus sheepdogs and foxhounds. 'I feel very proud about small achievements. I feel proud about rescuing sheep off crags.'

Dave Birkett's craggy features and strong hands are testament to a life spent on Lakeland rock faces

▲ *Dave Birkett, regarded as one of Britain's leading rock climbers, in the Langdales where he grew up*

Dave Birkett's work as a stonemason regularly takes him to the fells to repair dry stone walls

CHAPTER 10

JOHN RUSKIN

THE CURSE OF CELEBRITY wasn't invented in the twentieth century. One of the reasons for John Ruskin, the writer, patron of the arts and social critic, quitting London for the Lake District in 1872 was that he hoped to get away from unwanted attention.

At the time he swapped the capital for a house overlooking Coniston Water, Ruskin was so well known that he was being bothered by strangers. People would knock on his door to ask for his advice or to see his collection of paintings by J.M.W. Turner. 'By the time he moved to Brantwood, he was one of the most famous men in England,' says Professor Stephen Wildman, director of the Ruskin Library and Research Centre at Lancaster University. Ruskin also hated the fact that London had become so industrialised and he planned to escape from it all. He did what many people were doing at that time and have continued to do since: he headed to the Lake District for some peace and quiet, an inspiring view and the opportunity to get on with some work.

Ruskin is known as a Lake District writer – even though he was from London – and Brantwood, which was his home until his death in 1900, is open to the public to visit.

He had much in common with Beatrix Potter, another writer forever associated with the area: both were from London; both first encountered the Lake District as children while on family holidays; both later made their homes in the same area of the Lakes; and both became known internationally for their writing. There's no record of them meeting or speaking, although they were known to have been in the same room together, in 1884 at the Royal Academy in London. In her journal, the young Beatrix referred to Ruskin as looking ridiculous and having trouble with one of his trouser legs.

Interest in Ruskin has waxed and waned since his death. The complex nature of his private life means that television dramas and films tend to focus on scandal rather than his work. His marriage was annulled on the grounds of non-consummation and his wife went on to marry John Everett Millais, an artist at one time championed by Ruskin. Ruskin later developed a romantic obsession with Rose La Touche, whom he had first met when she was just a young girl. However, in Victorian England, Ruskin was primarily famous for his writing. By the beginning of the 1870s, his work included the startling art criticism of *Modern Painters*, which ran to five volumes; *The Seven Lamps of Architecture* and *The Stones of Venice*, which were major studies of architecture; and *Unto This Last*, which saw a shift in his interests towards working people, society and economics. He had had a selection of work published in the early 1860s when he was in his 40s, something that would have been highly unusual for a prose writer at that time. 'People who regarded themselves as well educated would have known about Ruskin and read Ruskin and probably would have had something [by him] on their shelves,' says Stephen Wildman. 'And he was in the newspapers a lot, speaking his mind, writing his letters and being known as an authority.' His influence continued after his death and his ideas have been cited by other famous thinkers including Marcel Proust, Leo Tolstoy, Mahatma Gandhi and the founders of the early Labour Party.

So Ruskin, famous but fed up, decided to move to the Lake District. However, fond of Cumbria as he was, it wasn't his only option. He also

John Ruskin left London to set up home at Brantwood, overlooking Coniston Water, partly to get away from overwhelming public attention

▲ *Guests who dined at Brantwood included Charles Darwin*

▼ *Brantwood provided Ruskin with the peace and quiet he needed*

loved the Alps and Stephen believes that given the choice between Chamonix and Coniston, he would have taken Chamonix, where he had tried – ultimately unsuccessfully – to live one winter. Having known the Lakes for many years, the area was a good second choice. And for someone who was still travelling regularly to London and Oxford, Coniston was also more accessible than Scotland, another place which he favoured. The Lake District was somewhere with which Ruskin had been familiar since childhood. He'd visited in 1824, 1826 and 1830, the last being an extended stay when he saw William Wordsworth for the first time. In a similar way to that in which – more than fifty years later – the young Beatrix Potter would be rude about him, Ruskin later wrote that he was 'rather disappointed in this gentleman's appearance, especially as he seemed to be asleep the greater part of the time. He seemed about 60. This gentleman possesses a long face and a large nose with a moderate assortment of grey hairs and two small grey eyes.'

The Lakes provided the source material for Ruskin's first published work. He was 10 when the poem 'On Skiddaw and Derwent-Water', based on his first two Lake District trips, was published by *The Spiritual Times*. He later worked on a longer poem in rhyming couplets which was called 'Iteriad' or 'Three Weeks among the Lakes'. Forty years later, Ruskin was to make his home in the area which had made such an impression on him.

It's sometimes said that Ruskin bought Brantwood, for £1,500, 'sight unseen', but that doesn't mean that he purchased the house in 1871 without knowing anything about it. 'It's an exaggeration really because although he didn't view it in the way we would now view a house with an estate agent, he knew where it was,' says Stephen. 'He must have passed it or knew where the site was because there's a drawing of Coniston Old Man he did from that side of the lake when he was 19.' The outlook was a large part of what attracted Ruskin to the property. He wrote to an American friend that it was 'on the whole the finest view I know in Cumberland or Lancashire with the sunset visible …'. Stephen says: 'The view was the point. He wouldn't have bought another house in Coniston or in Ambleside or Keswick; he knew that view was there.'

The view partly explains why he left a beautifully appointed house in London to buy a smaller home in poor repair. Before moving in during 1872, Ruskin added a turret to his bedroom, all the better to admire the view, and built an extension for a dining room. He also built a cottage for his valet which was about the same size as the house, indicating the type of relationship he had with people who worked for him. Howard Hull, the director of Brantwood and the Ruskin Foundation, believes that Ruskin didn't plan to make any more alterations to his new home. 'I have a feeling Ruskin intended to stop there,' he says. His intention was to live simply; although he'd inherited a huge sum from his father – between £15 million and £20 million in today's money – he was critical of those who believed that money and wealth were synonymous and coined the phrase 'there is no wealth but life' to summarise his position. However, Brantwood was gradually expanded into the substantial property that it is today. A major reason for this was the input of Ruskin's cousin, Joan Severn. After six years at Coniston, Ruskin suffered his first breakdown and Joan came to live with him, bringing her husband, Arthur and the first of their five children. Brantwood then became a building site for much of Ruskin's life as it was continually expanded to accommodate the children – who were educated there – and the household that was required to look after everyone.

Howard says that, by and large, Brantwood and Coniston helped Ruskin achieve the type of lifestyle he wanted. Although he'd quit London (while retaining a room in the capital), his fame meant that he remained of interest to the public. Pictures of Brantwood were popular and tourists bought prints and postcards of the view of the house from across Coniston Water. Ruskin became even more famous after he'd moved to Coniston because of his appointment as the first Slade Professor of Fine Art at Oxford University in 1870. Howard says: 'He travelled backwards and forwards from here to Oxford when he became much more of a celebrity than he was in the 1860s.' However, visitors weren't likely to knock on the

After moving to Brantwood, Ruskin added a turret to his bedroom, all the better to admire the view across Coniston Water

Despite Ruskin's desire to avoid public attention, he allowed his signature to be used on a number of souvenirs

door, he says: 'The ordinary tourist would go past on the lane and look up.' Joan managed to keep people at bay and most requests to see 'the professor' were refused. Despite Ruskin's need to get away from the public and Joan's assistance in maintaining his privacy, one or both of them was responsible for licensing the use of Ruskin's signature on a number of souvenirs, including a tea cup and saucer and a coffee cup, examples of which are on display at Brantwood. He also allowed photographers to take his picture. It also wasn't strictly accurate to say that Ruskin had swapped industrialised London for a bucolic Coniston; the village was and continues to be a proper working place and was more industrialised in the late nineteenth century than it is now. 'He wasn't trying to be a hermit; he just wanted to be alone, he wanted not to be bothered by people, in a very nice place and Coniston fitted the bill with a wonderful view,' says Stephen Wildman. 'You have to remember there was Coniston copper mining so it was noisier than you imagine.' Tourism was also coming to the Lake District and the village wasn't unaffected. In 1854, the Furness Railway

built a branch line to Coniston to service the mines and it was also used by tourists, who took to the lake in the steam yacht *Gondola*.

Ruskin's life at Brantwood revolved around his work and his writing. House guests were more likely to be family friends than famous people. One well-known dinner guest was Charles Darwin, whose visit was apparently arranged by his wife, Emma, an admirer of Ruskin. She hoped that her husband and Ruskin might talk about Darwin's loss of faith and this would help him, although there's no evidence that this happened. Ruskin also liked putting some of his ideas into practice at Brantwood; in fact it became a type of laboratory for his theories about gardening, land husbandry and water management. He experimented with a moorland garden, where he created two small reservoirs and built an ice house to supply ice for when people in the village were sick. House guests would be invited on to the estate to work with him. He drew a comical sketch of himself leading a working party up a steep hill, indicating that he did, in fact, have a sense of humour.

Stephen Wildman says that visits to Ruskin's home wouldn't have been about relaxation: 'He didn't like wasting time in doing nothing; you didn't get much idle chatter at Brantwood. If you were invited you had things to do; invariably there would be readings from Walter Scott's novels, whether you wanted them or not. There might be a little piano playing or he would pass round his rocks for you to look at or comment on. There wasn't much in the way of light entertainment.' There was no electricity at the house but there was running water from the fell.

Although Ruskin remained a man of faith, he didn't enjoy church attendance and wasn't a regular worshipper at St Andrew's in the village, much to the annoyance of the vicar, Charles Chapman. Stephen Wildman says: 'Chapman was really quite put out – here was one of the most famous men in England but [he] didn't go to church. I think Ruskin didn't want to waste an entire Sunday morning being bored.' Ruskin did make financial contributions to village life but they were more likely to be for the school, where he provided items such as a simplified map of the constellations. He also helped to support projects such as the revival of the Langdale linen industry.

Ruskin's life at Brantwood revolved around his study, where he worked and wrote

Stories have circulated about the end of Ruskin's life, which say that when he was gripped by the mania or temporary madness that afflicted his later years, he would 'escape' from his carers at Brantwood, fly across the lake in his rowing boat, *Jumping Jenny*, and charge up Coniston Old Man before anyone had noticed he'd gone. The truth is less dramatic. For a start, his cousin Joan would have been aware of him showing signs of an episode of illness and would have been able to stop him from going out on his own. However, Ruskin was more than capable of rowing across Coniston Water and climbing the Old Man – the mountain which was the highest point in the old county of Lancashire and which he had come to regard as a sort of friend. 'Getting up early, rowing across to the Old Man and coming back before breakfast would be a good way of starting the day, especially if he came back with a plant or a rock he could draw,' explains Stephen Wildman. Howard Hull agrees that Ruskin loved to be outdoors and walked a great deal in his early years at Brantwood. Although there's no evidence that he ever reached the summit of the Old Man, he knew the countryside extremely well and wrote about it extensively. 'Ruskin did love to row in rough water in *Jumping Jenny* but I don't imagine he did it a great deal – he was quite a good age,' he says. 'The boat doesn't row that well. I don't think he would have made enormous headway.'

The Lake District has provided inspiration for artists, poets, writers and thinkers for centuries but Ruskin didn't need Coniston to be able to write what he did. 'It was inspirational in practical ways,' says Stephen. 'So when he's writing about a subject, if he happens to look out of the window and sees something, that becomes part of his writing. It's not really the other way round. He doesn't need to go wandering about like Wordsworth for inspiration.' While he was living at Brantwood, Ruskin wrote books about geology, flowers and birds. Howard Hull agrees that he could have penned them wherever he'd been living. However, they would have been different because of the way in which Ruskin wrote – he put his situation, wherever he happened to be at the time of writing, at the centre of his descriptions and so took the reader with him, seeing through his eyes both the inspiration itself and the source of that inspiration. Howard also believes that Brantwood helped Ruskin to be happy:

'Brantwood actually did what Ruskin came to Brantwood for, in that it gave him peace and a return to the natural world, which was like a return to the roots of his inspiration.' His doomed feelings for Rose La Touche, who died in 1875 aged 27, affected him deeply. 'It cast a big shadow over everything for Ruskin,' says Howard. 'He was immersed in his work to a degree. I think that's why Brantwood represented an escape from that side of things and gave him the opportunity to find something very happy and uncomplicated by comparison.'

There is an abiding image of him as an unhappy figure during the last ten years of his life when he ceased to write and drifted into old age but Howard sees this period differently: 'I think he was actually at peace. He might have returned to a sort of second childhood in the process.' Ruskin died in 1900. Despite St Andrew's church being snubbed during his life and a funeral and burial at Westminster Abbey being offered, Joan said that Ruskin had wanted to be interred in the village. His grave, at St Andrew's, is still a place of pilgrimage today. Ruskin's celebrity continued after his death. The press coverage of his funeral and the debate about his life that followed were huge and were only exceeded by those for Queen Victoria the following year. Although he'd already produced a lot of his great work by the time he moved to Coniston, his early years at Brantwood were productive.

Howard says: 'He wrote a lot of books here, some beautiful books, not least of which is the most read of Ruskin's books and the most loved by ordinary people, which is his autobiography, *Praeterita*. All of that was written here, so writing was a key part of his life and achievement at Brantwood.' When he first bought the house, Ruskin, writing to his American friend, made a prediction about life in Coniston that was fulfilled: '... [h]ere I have rocks, streams, fresh air, and for the first time in my life, the rest of the proposed home.'

Although he didn't attend services at St Andrew's church in Coniston, it was chosen as his final resting place

CHAPTER 11

THE HIGH PASSES OF WRYNOSE AND HARDKNOTT

HARRY BERGER can remember the first time he came over Wrynose and Hardknott passes into the Eskdale Valley. He'd got as far as Elterwater, close to the start of Wrynose and had twenty minutes to reach his appointment. It was his first encounter with the physical geography of the passes and like many before him, he found that the contours of a map entirely failed to capture the reality of the roads. As Harry puts it: 'It doesn't matter how many circles you put on a map, you don't realise how steep it is.' After negotiating his way up and down the steep ascents and descents and round the hairpin bends to the valley, he had already written it off as a place where he might invest in a pub business:

I did Wrynose, I was following a snail and I overtook him and I came down the [Hardknott] pass and thought forget it, I might as well go home, nobody's ever going to come here. I walked into The Boot Inn and it was heaving – there were about 100 people in there in the middle of June on a Tuesday. I turned round and said, 'Where the hell has everybody come from?'

He had counted only four cars in the car park: 'They had come off the train, they had come off the fells, come from everywhere.' Not only was it Harry's first encounter with Wrynose and Hardknott but he says it was also the first and last time he overtook someone on the stretch of road. That was in June 1998 and later that year Harry, his wife Paddington and their two children moved to The Boot Inn. They now own and run the

Woolpack Inn, further along the valley. Harry says he never wants to leave Eskdale but he's had to adapt to the unique landscape, explaining that you must accept you're a long way from anywhere else. During the tourist season you need to allow even more time to get to your destination and it's often quicker to cycle than to drive.

Harry's first experience of driving over Wrynose and Hardknott isn't unusual. The twin passes are often crossed on the same journey – from Little Langdale to Eskdale – but in his book, *Wainwright on the Lakeland Mountain Passes*, the guidebook author Alfred Wainwright warns that drivers who have come over Wrynose from the east must expect 'a much stiffer climb' over Hardknott and should approach it with 'the utmost concentration'. In fact, Wainwright goes so far as to say that of the seven mountain passes in the Lakes which are crossed by roads, Hardknott is the 'most notorious' and challenges the skill and nerve of car drivers. Hardknott is often described as the most difficult road in Britain. It begins to climb, Wainwright says, innocuously from Cockley Beck Bridge but, 'soon springs to life in a heart-stopping series of sharp and narrow hairpin bends with a gradient of 1 in 3'. Once over the pass, there is a steep and awkward corner to navigate before the long route down to the valley. Wrynose is only a little less daunting and perhaps seems an easier route, just because it's located next to Hardknott. Sportspeople who want to test their limits love the two passes and hold events over the punishing terrains through the year. The best known is the Fred Whitton Challenge, a 112-mile cycling event around the Lake District. The event's website calls Hardknott the daddy of all the climbs and is full of warnings about

Hardknott Pass is known as one of Britain's most challenging roads

the ascents and descents on both passes, urging riders to watch their speeds if they don't want to come off the road and find themselves in need of an ambulance.

Unwitting motorists are caught out by the tricky terrain. Harry says he's put his car on its roof in the winter. On one particular bend, the driver of a lorry and trailer jackknifed the vehicle, which was stuck there for four days. Locals duly named the bend after the supermarket which had sent out the unfortunate lorry. Harry and Paddington encourage first-time visitors not to follow their sat navs, which would take them to the Woolpack via Ambleside and then Wrynose and Hardknott but to follow alternative routes from the north and the south. By all means try the roads at a leisurely pace during the holiday, they advise but don't venture on to them for the first time in the dark or bad weather. There's a reason rally cars are tested on Hardknott, says Harry: 'We tell everybody, unless you know it, do not follow your sat nav. Unless you know the road, don't come that way. You've got to be prepared for it. If you've never driven it, you've got to think about it to go and do it.' Well-prepared drivers are rewarded for their efforts: 'But the views when you're up there, they're quite incredible. On a clear day you can see the Isle of Man. On an entirely clear evening you can see the flashes out in the Irish Sea when they're burning the gas off the oil rigs.'

Since moving to the valley, Harry and Paddington have made the most of being in the community. Harry has helped clear the passes of snow, earning the thanks of cyclists. There is an 'unbelievable pride' that goes with living in the valley, plus a feeling of responsibility and they look after the landscape by sticking to environmental principles in their businesses. There's also pride in being situated at the end of two of the most challenging roads most of us are likely to drive. Harry says: 'The description that we've coined for them – Hardknott and Wrynose – is they're Britain's or England's two most outrageous roads. They're not necessarily the steepest or highest but they're the most outrageous.'

Wrynose and Hardknott have seen their fair share of stories and adventures. In his book *English Lake Country*, published in 1969, the farmer Dudley Hoys recounts a romance that took place against the

▲ *The beginning of Hardknott Pass – described by Alfred Wainwright as 'a heart-stopping series of sharp and narrow hairpin bends'*

▼ *Harry Berger warns first-time visitors to his pub in Eskdale not to attempt Hardknott and Wrynose passes until they're familiar with the landscape*

Drivers make their way along the steeply climbing Wrynose Pass

backdrop of the two passes. A respected shepherd, who was known as an enthusiastic walker, worked at the head of Eskdale but fell in love with a young woman in Little Langdale. Without a car, he took it upon himself to walk the 9 miles or 14km over Hardknott and Wrynose two or three times a week. The author calculated that he began at an altitude of 300ft (91m), ascended to 1,290ft (393m), descended to 750ft (229m), ascended to 1,280ft (390m) and descended to 300ft. Sadly, after six months of this, the shepherd was turned down. Dudley Hoys speculates that he lost out to someone with a sports car. There are other stories about the origins of the name Wrynose, said variously to be 'vreini hals' or the pass of the stallion, where the animals would fall and break their teeth, or 'raven hause', the home of the raven. Torrential rain would cause an avalanche from time to time, such as in 1966 when the scree and boulder which tore down the fell took off a slice of road. Dudley Hoys also recounts a sad story of a man who set off one Sunday morning to drive from a hotel in Langdale over the passes and on to Wasdale Head, where he never arrived. No trace of him was found until the Thursday evening, when a local man drove over Hardknott summit and spotted a car, with its windows covered in hail and snow. The next morning, Dudley joined the police to look for the man while intermittent blizzards of snow swirled around them. They thought the man had left his car for a stroll, fallen into a gully and died from exposure. A week after the motorist had set off, information came from his sister that he was fond of Esk Hause, a 760m or 2,500ft plateau which is known as a confusing spot for walkers. The search moved to that area. It would have taken the man approximately two hours to reach Esk Hause from the summit of Harknott and it was never known if he'd made it, as his body was found lower down on a ridge of Esk Pike. Dudley writes that the rescue party hoped he'd died quickly.

Just below Hardknott summit lies the remains of a Roman fort, located there to protect convoys on their way from Ambleside to Ravenglass. It was the scene of more recent battles, when, in the 1930s, the Forestry Commission acquired more than 7,000 acres of land and proposed to establish Hardknott Forest Park. In his book *Lakeland Valleys*, Robert Gambles records how there was a public outcry about the possibility of

Farmer Kevin Wrathall and his daughter, Abby, at Cockley Beck Farm, which was built at the junction of Wrynose and Hardknott Passes

the uplands being submerged in a 'sea of conifers', as had happened elsewhere in the Lake District. A petition against further State Forests in the Lake District was signed by 13,000 people, the National Trust and Friends of the Lake District weighed in and the forest was never planted.

Cockley Beck farmhouse was built in the late 1860s and stands at the point where the feet of the two passes meet. Today it belongs to the National Trust and is occupied by farmer Kevin Wrathall, his partner Sandra Swainson and their two daughters. Kevin has experienced his share of bad weather but in years gone by it could be even more extreme. In *English Lake Country*, Dudley Hoys records how, in early 1947, the family at the farm was cut off by huge drifts of snow. Once it started

Motorists give way to native Herdwicks at Wrynose Bottom

to thaw and Dudley made his way over to the farm, he was greeted by the farmer's wife who told him that he was the first person, outside her own family, that she'd seen for six weeks. Kevin and Sandra have, in fact, come to appreciate winter because of the peace and quiet that they enjoy. Tourism has meant that the summer brings a constant stream of people to their home. 'I prefer the winter to the summer when people come knocking on the door,' says Kevin. 'They've blown a tyre off or they're lost, "can we borrow your toilet", "can we have a drink". If it's an emergency I don't mind at all but if it's just changing their tyre they should be able to get on and do it.' Modern reliance on mobile phones means that when visitors find themselves without a signal, they're flummoxed. The callers come steadily through the week with a peak at weekends. Stranded motorists had been racking up expensive calls on the Cockley Beck phone. A final straw was a £9 call for which the visitor had left a contribution of £1. Eventually, Kevin and Sandra were forced to put a sign on the door letting people know that they will need to pay £5 for a phone call. One or two of Kevin's experiences would have tested anybody's patience, such as when some young walkers who'd bitten off more than they could chew during an expedition came calling. 'We had some lads knock on the door, quarter past four in the morning. They said they were tired, they were a long way from anywhere and would I take them over to Langdale.' Kevin's response isn't recorded. It's little wonder that Kevin and Sandra prefer the winter, whatever the weather might throw at them: 'You don't get the same hassles and same bother – you might see five or six cars going past through the winter – in the summer it's just a constant line of traffic.' Kevin is there for people in need: 'You can see it on their faces if it's a real emergency; somebody's come off a push bike, I wouldn't be charging them a fiver.'

For Kevin, taking on Cockley Beck was an opportunity for the former self-employed farm worker to run a decent fell farm with its own Herdwick flock. He'd helped the previous farmer and so he knew what to expect from the farm and from the winters. He and Sandra also rent out a holiday cottage. Their nearest neighbour is about a mile down the road and it's an 11-mile drive to Broughton-in-Furness village or 10 miles to the town of Ambleside. There's no TV signal but they can watch via a satellite service which also provides internet access. Kevin says he and the family just get on with life on the farm. When his eldest daughter, Holly, was at nursery, Sandra drove 48 miles each time she dropped her off, returned home and then went to collect her again. Things are easier now that Holly travels to school in a taxi, which also picks up another little girl. The winter weather can be harsh and Kevin has had to dig through snowdrifts but in early 2013, when some Lakeland farmers lost 200 sheep to snow, Kevin counted himself lucky that his losses were in the teens. There is plenty of Lake District rain and he jokes: 'We get three months of rain and nine months of bad weather.' There are fewer farmers than there once were but Kevin says they still muck in to help one another at hay time or to fetch sheep from the fells. If someone's tractor breaks they can borrow their neighbour's. Kevin enjoys being away from it all: Cockley Beck is only 4 miles from the summit of Scafell Pike and although it's not the most popular route to England's highest peak, walkers who go that way are likely to be rewarded by having the landscape to themselves. For Kevin, the best thing about living at Cockley Beck is the satisfaction of a job well done, when he sells his lambs and gets a good price: 'You're here to farm sheep and produce sheep and if you've done it well and you get a nice price for them it's always quite rewarding. You just get on with what you're doing.' Kevin is at Cockley Beck through choice: 'It's one of those places, if you didn't like it you would find somewhere else. I couldn't do it just to make money; you've got to enjoy it. It does test you from time to time. Once you've come through it, you can look back on it and even smile.'

CHAPTER 12

CONISTON WATER

WINDERMERE MAY be larger and Wastwater is deeper but Coniston Water is the lake with the stories to tell. Its 5-mile long surface, which can be mirror-like or choppy – often in quick succession – has been the scene of many dramatic moments and its depths have held their fair share of secrets.

Coniston's most famous story is that captured in grainy black and white film footage taken on 4 January 1967, when the speed record-breaker Donald Campbell took off from the lake in his jet-powered hydroplane, Bluebird K7, which somersaulted and crashed back on the water, sinking beneath its surface and settling on the lake bed. Many people who are old enough to remember the wintry day can recall learning of the accident and few who have watched the evocative footage have remained unmoved. Following the crash, divers were unable to find the speed hero's body and so both the skipper and his craft lay undisturbed for more than thirty-four years.

On that day, Britain lost one of its heroes, a record-breaker who had pushed the boundaries on both land and water. Campbell, who had taken on the speed record mantle from his father, Sir Malcolm Campbell, remains the only person to have captured the land and water world speed records in the same year, which he did in 1964. When he died, he was trying to push Bluebird K7, a craft which was regarded by some as past her prime, to 300mph, to better his own record of 276.33mph and to keep it in British hands. Although, arguably, at the time of his death his glory days were already behind him, he was still a national figure, a handsome man and hero to many. His loss was felt at home and around the world. For his only child, Gina Campbell, his death was devastating and its effects long lasting. Not only was Gina left fatherless at age 17 but the accident also saw her become the keeper of her father's legacy, a role that must have been a blessing and also a curse over the years. And although Gina has never lived in Coniston and neither of her parents was from the area, her father's death also left her with a lifelong connection to the village and Coniston Water. When she was finally able to bury her father, in 2001, it was Coniston churchyard which she chose as his resting place.

Speaking at her home near Leeds in December 2013, Gina recalled one of her first visits to Coniston. It was 1956 and Donald had set a new world record of 225.63mph in Bluebird on 19 September – which was also Gina's seventh birthday. She says: 'I just remember dad breaking the record on my birthday and somebody thrusting a microphone underneath my nose.' The journalist asked Gina if the record was the very best present she could have asked for: 'I said "Oh no, I would much rather have a pony."' Decades later, it's easy to laugh at this exchange but it was an early example of how Gina has been a source of fascination for journalists and for her father's fans and followers. A former power boater herself – she's held two women's world water speed records – Gina is primarily known as the keeper of the Campbell flame. Hugely proud of her father's achievements and bereaved at a young age, it must have been difficult for her to continually be asked about the accident which killed her dad. However, somehow she became used to dealing with the fallout from the crash. In 2001, that fallout was to take a surprising turn.

A mirror-calm Coniston Water

Gina Campbell's record-breaking family includes her grandfather, Sir Malcolm Campbell and father, Donald Campbell

Over the years, when she was back in Coniston, Gina says she found it difficult to approach the edge of the lake, knowing that her father's remains were still at the bottom. Her feelings about Coniston Water often manifested themselves in physical symptoms and she'd regularly find herself rushing off to be sick. For the twentieth anniversary of the crash, Gina agreed to take part in the remake of a documentary called *The Price of a Record*, presented by Melvyn Bragg. Against what she says was her better judgement – she says it would have felt as if she was walking on her father's grave – Gina agreed to drive a boat up Coniston Water, following the measured mile which Donald took when he was attempting his records. However, every time they tried to film the footage,

the weather suddenly turned to black skies, fierce winds and rain and the boat had to be taken off the water. After this had happened three times, Melvyn told Gina he felt somebody didn't want them on the lake. Gina believes it was her dad's influence at work and he was saying, 'Bugger off, this is my domain'. 'It just didn't feel right to me,' she says.

It was the mid-1990s when Gina first heard from an amateur diver called Bill Smith who told her he had found her father's boat. Local people said at the time that they'd known all along where the boat had sunk and that it had, in actual fact, never been lost. However, diving and underwater technology had moved on during the thirty years Bluebird had been at the bottom of the lake and it was felt that the boat would now be vulnerable to divers who might be tempted to take a piece of the famous craft. Against the background of those concerns, the wreckage of the boat – still clearly recognisable as Bluebird – was recovered from the lake in March 2001 in a blaze of newspaper headlines. Once the boat was out, it followed that the skipper should be found and in May that year, the same divers returned and brought up Donald's remains. Gina says that she was asked if there was anything else the divers should look for. 'I said, "Yes, he will have had a St Christopher round his neck on a cord."' Incredibly, the divers found the St Christopher, engraved 'To Donald, From Daddy, Nov 1940', plus his lighter and the loose change that had been in his pocket. Together with Mr Whoppit, Donald's teddy bear mascot, which had been with him in Bluebird and floated to the surface following the accident, the items are a poignant set of unique keepsakes. Gina was devastated when she was later to lose the St Christopher, although it was eventually found in her garden, to her immense relief. She was finally able to hold her dad's funeral, at St Andrew's church in Coniston, on 12 September 2001, the day after the terrorist attacks on the twin towers of the World Trade Center in New York. He was buried in the graveyard across the road from the church and such are the numbers of people who still want to pay their respects that a path has been specially constructed to lead to the grave.

Since burying her dad, Gina says the symptoms that afflicted her over the years when she visited Coniston have lessened: 'I think, with a lot of people, when you're uneasy the first thing that's affected is the old tummy. That really had an impact on me – and I don't have that anymore.' Bluebird is meanwhile being restored to her 1967 condition and is ultimately destined to be displayed at the village's Ruskin Museum. Although Gina no longer experiences physical symptoms when she visits Coniston, the village and the lake will always conjure up strong feelings: 'I always found it spooky, I will always find it spooky, there's no point in trying to pretend not because I can't go up there with great gales of joy. Yes, my father had some of his finest hours there but also it's where he died.' And yet she's clear that the manner of her father's death has immortalised his memory. His own father, Sir Malcolm Campbell, died following a stroke and Donald had hated to see him so diminished. At least his own death, at the controls of Bluebird, had spared Donald a similar decline. Gina believes that if her dad had died of old age, in his 90s, there would have been a few lines in a newspaper recording his passing. By going out in a blaze of glory, he was assured a place in history and a permanent link with the lake where he met his end. People still tell Gina they can remember where they were when they heard about her father's accident. As she puts it: 'If he had not died like that, he would have disappeared into oblivion. He would have just been another world water speed record holder. That's really quite ironic and Coniston is part and parcel of that.'

The story of Sir Malcolm and Donald's exploits on the lake forms part of a special 'Campbells on Coniston' cruise, operated by the boat company Coniston Launch. The firm also runs a 'Swallows and Amazons' cruise, which invites visitors to identify the real-life locations which inspired fictional places written about by Arthur Ransome, the journalist and novelist. Ransome became world-famous for his *Swallows and Amazons* series of children's books, which were published in the 1930s and '40s. Vicky Slowe, the curator of the Ruskin Museum in the village, has spent more than twenty years interpreting the history of Coniston for visitors. According to Vicky, Ransome first came to Coniston as a young boy when his father, Cyril, brought his family from Leeds to the Lake District on holiday. Cyril had been corresponding with W.G. Collingwood, a writer and artist who was also secretary to John Ruskin, the great Victorian art

Divers who recovered Donald Campbell's body from Coniston Water in 2001 also retrieved his engraved lighter and St Christopher medallion and loose change

*5-mile-long Coniston Water attracted the speed record-breaker
Donald Campbell and the writers John Ruskin and Arthur Ransome*

critic and sage. Cyril arranged for his family to meet Collingwood for a picnic on Peel Island on the lake. Arthur was apparently quite thrilled by this because, as a young boy, his favourite book had been Collingwood's Norse tale *Thorstein of the Mere*. Something about this meeting on an island appears to have lodged in Ransome's mind. In later life, Ransome grew close to Collingwood and his family and they taught him to sail in a boat called *Swallow*. Both Windermere – where Arthur had gone to school – and Coniston provided fictional locations for *Swallows and Amazons*. On Coniston, Peel Island is thought to be Wild Cat Island while Allan Tarn, at the southern end of the lake, is believed to be the fictional Octopus Lagoon. Meanwhile, the mountain which the children dub Kanchenjunga is based on Coniston Old Man. Arthur spent many holidays in the area and eventually returned to live in the Lake District. Fans of the author have been raising funds with the aim of building a centre in the Lakes dedicated to his work.

Along with Ransome and Campbell, John Ruskin is the third man who will forever be associated with Coniston Water. No longer a household name, at one time Ruskin was one of the most famous men in the country. In 1872, he moved to a house called Brantwood, with views over the lake to the village and across to Coniston Old Man and lived there until his death in 1900. A visionary art critic, he later turned his attention to social issues and his ideas and thinking have proved hugely influential on figures such as Mahatma Gandhi and social developments including the National Trust, the NHS and public libraries. Like Arthur Ransome, John Ruskin first came to the Lake District on holiday as a child. He moved to Coniston from London in search of peace and quiet and to get away from the attention he attracted in the capital. Although he suffered a series of breakdowns, his years at Brantwood did bring him some of the peace that he craved and his work during that period included his autobiography. Like Campbell, he is buried at St Andrew's church and his grave is still sought out by his followers.

Coniston doesn't have the chocolate box looks of other Lake District villages and has remained a working village with the feel of a real community. Its residents don't mind getting stuck in and volunteering if there's a service under threat or money needs to be raised for a good cause. It's surrounded by high peaks, including Coniston Old Man, which was the highest point in Lancashire before the local government reorganisation of 1974 relocated the village in the newly formed Cumbria. The Ruskin Museum's Vicky Slowe points out that for some people, the proximity of the surrounding mountains gives Coniston a particular grandeur. Vicky says that Coniston Water has always lent itself to record-breaking and it's now home to the annual Coniston Power Boat Records Week. In 1939, with war looming, Donald Campbell's father, Sir Malcolm, was reluctant to travel to the Continent and decided to stage a record attempt in the Lake District. Vicky says that he chose Coniston partly because of its physical features and also because it wasn't Windermere, where Sir Henry Segrave, his contemporary and fellow record-breaker, had crashed and later died. 'I think all racing people were pretty superstitious so Sir Malcolm wouldn't have anything to do with Windermere,' says Vicky. 'Derwentwater and Bassenthwaite are too shallow, Ullswater has a great kink in it but Coniston is straight, it's deep, its two islands are to the side.' Donald also came to favour Coniston, where he had made friends and where he was welcomed back each time he came on a record-breaking mission. When Gina buried her dad, she chose a plot as close as possible to Connie Robinson, who had put him up at The Sun hotel in the village and had become a good friend. Coniston and its lake played a huge part in the life and careers of Donald Campbell, Arthur Ransome and John Ruskin. Each found that Coniston Water helped them in their work, providing a calming influence, fuelling their imaginations and allowing them to fulfil their destinies. Donald experienced Coniston Water's mirror-calm surface but he also knew how violently it can be whipped up by the weather and such conditions caused him many problems during the winter of 1966 and 1967 during his final record-breaking bid. He had an ambivalent relationship with the lake but the village and its inhabitants always made him welcome and have provided him with his final resting place. Vicky Slowe says: 'He frequently called the lake a bitch because the weather conditions were so changeable – but from what one can make out, he felt very much at home in Coniston.'

Coniston Water made international headlines following Donald Campbell's fatal accident in Bluebird in January 1967

Trees on Coniston Water's eastern shore

ABOUT THE AUTHORS

MICHAELA ROBINSON-TATE trained as a newspaper journalist. She has worked in newspapers, radio and magazines in north Lancashire and Cumbria since 1993 and is currently senior writer with *Cumbria Life* magazine. *Lake District Icons* is her first book.

PHIL RIGBY has been a professional press photographer for twenty-six years and he is now picture editor at CN Magazines with responsibility for three titles, including *Cumbria Life*. An experienced rock climber and member of the Fell & Rock Climbing Club, he has contributed to a series of specialist Lake District climbing guides.

The authors